WHO WINS WARS

ALSO BY ML CAVANAUGH

Best Scar Wins: How You Can Be More Than You Were Before

Winning Westeros: How Game of Thrones
Explains Modern Military Conflict
(with John Amble, Max Brooks, and Jaym Gates)

Strategy Strikes Back: How Star Wars *Explains Modern Military Conflict*
(with John Amble, Max Brooks, and Jaym Gates)

WHO WINS WARS

Lessons in Leadership, Power, and Supreme Command from Washington, Grant, and Eisenhower

ML CAVANAUGH,

Lt. Col. US Army, Ret.

Matt Holt Books

An Imprint of BenBella Books, Inc.

Dallas, TX

Matt Holt is an imprint of BenBella Books, Inc.
BenBella Books, Inc.
8080 N. Central Expressway
Suite 1700
Dallas, TX 75206
benbellabooks.com
Send feedback to feedback@benbellabooks.com

Matt Holt and *BenBella* are federally registered trademarks.

Printed in the United States of America
10 9 8 7 6 5 4 3 2 1

Library of Congress Control Number: 2026000725
ISBN 9781637749180 (hardcover)
ISBN 9781637749197 (electronic)

Editing by Katie Dickman
Copyediting by James Fraleigh
Proofreading by Lisa Story and Ashley Casteel
Indexing by WordCo. Indexing Services
Text design and composition by Aaron Edmiston
Cover design by Jason Arias
Cover image courtesy of the Library of Congress
Printed by Lake Book Manufacturing

For Colin S. Gray

CONTENTS

Part I: The Pursuit of Success

Part II: How Washington Won

Part III: How Grant Won

Part IV: How Eisenhower Won

Part V: The Art of the Better Decision

Dolor hic tibi proderit olim

—Ovid

Foreword

JAMES STAVRIDIS, ADMIRAL, US NAVY (RET.)

He wanted to understand how wars are won.

Having fought in the biggest war there ever was, Rear Admiral J. C. Wylie spent the early years of the Cold War writing and refining the ideas that later became his classic book, *Military Strategy: A General Theory of Power Control*. He focused on "warfare, not battles," and the "whole of the thing," instead of "counting the bullets or tracing the route of the *n*th division on a large-scale map."[*]

Wylie lamented that while several "other fields of human activities" had been exhaustively researched,

> only the tremendous social upheaval of war itself has never really been studied with a fundamental and systematic objectivity that would lead the student (and the practitioner) to recognize and better understand a basic pattern of thought, a theory, that did

---

[*] J. C. Wylie, *Military Strategy: A General Theory of Power Control* (Naval Institute Press, 1989, originally published 1967), 12.

or could influence the conduct of war, influence the basic matter of whether or not a people or a nation might survive.[*]

Wylie acknowledged previous theorists, like Clausewitz and Mahan, had "studied and juggled around the detailed specifics or statistics of war"—yet "none of them has set himself the task of trying to make a little clearer why wars are managed the way they are." Wylie wanted us to "understand a little better the paths that are followed by the strategic mind at work."[†]

Six decades and many more wars later, Wylie's challenge has been met and answered. Matt Cavanaugh's *Who Wins Wars* is the best book on American supreme command I've seen in a long time. This is the story Wylie sought—the patterns of thought that led to strategic success.

Even better is what it can tell us about strategic leadership. The lessons in this book transcend time and place. It turns out the "art of the better decision," as Matt calls it, travels far beyond the battlefield to other places demanding superior strategic leadership—like schools, hospitals, our capitals and cities, our places of worship, our small businesses and boardrooms, in dugouts, and on sidelines. The stakes may not be quite so high here, but for those locked in competition, the dynamics are largely the same.

As a former Supreme Allied Commander Europe, throughout my career and after, I've always believed people come first. The right team, led well, can do nearly anything. Which is why I can see this book's got just the right aim in finding out *how* wars are won—by starting with *who* wins them.

---

[*] Wylie, 8–9.
[†] Wylie, 8–9.

Author's Note

While rooted in historical examples of superior performance, this is not a history book, nor is it written for a purely academic audience.[*]

It is written instead for strategic leaders of all stripes. The ones who want access to the minds and secrets of the strategic leaders who won the wars that mattered most.

It is not for those who aim to say, as tactical generals once did, "The day is ours." It is instead for those who aim higher, farther, longer. The strategic leaders who want to claim the future as ours.

It is for those who want to win the wars to come, the wars that matter, the wars that must be won.

---

[*] For those interested in such a version of this project, with a fuller reference list, please consult the University of Reading (UK) PhD archives (Matthew L. Cavanaugh, "On Supreme Command: The Characteristics of Successful American Generals at War," PhD diss., University of Reading, 2018, https://doi.org/10.48683/1926.00082827).

NOT ALL GENERALS ARE CREATED EQUAL

Just how do you recognize a great general?
—Historian T. Harry Williams

Not all generals are created equal.* Most are adequate. Some are rotten. A few, perhaps very few, are superior. This book is about what distinguishes these winning generals in a crucial subset of strategic leaders—supreme commanders at war. The supreme commander is charged with ultimate responsibility for a country's strategic performance at war.[1] They are the peak we will study to better understand the mountain.

Despite the obvious significance of their leadership, this type of strategic leader has largely evaded real scrutiny. Within the uniformed military, at least, it seems there's good reason this is so.

---

* Reader's note: This book will occasionally deploy the generic term "general" as a catchall simplification for any individual that's attained one of the ranks associated with being a military general or flag-level officer, including those in other military services (i.e., "admiral," "air vice marshal," and "commodore"). It will also, when appropriate, use specific ranks (e.g., "lieutenant general").

Though I served in the US Army for 25 years, in combat and as a staff officer and award-winning senior Strategist for over half that period, it took me a while to come to the conclusion that generals are fallible. The more junior you are in uniform, the more military culture encourages extreme deference to authority (especially when that authority wears several stars on its collar). So, you're conditioned to go along with whatever "the boss" says. Don't ask questions—the general knows better.

To be fair, this often makes sense, on the logic that someone at the totem pole's top sees the bigger picture. The general's got the better view.

But that's not always true, and I started to sense this in 2006 after returning from my second year-long tour of duty in Iraq. I fought under then-colonel H. R. McMaster and witnessed exceptional counterinsurgency strategic leadership.[2] McMaster wasn't flawless, but he did the big things better than our adversaries in northern Iraq. For our unit's successes, McMaster earned praise—high, far, and wide.[3] It was well known, however, that to achieve those gains, McMaster prodded the generals senior to him. And so, despite his clear achievements and sterling record, he was passed over for promotion to his first general's star twice. In the end, this military officer, who would later rise to the top of the American national security establishment, only got his first star after extraordinary outside intervention (by General David Petraeus).

How could such an obviously well-qualified individual have trouble making the jump to general? Exactly what does it take to be a general? Or, for that matter, what counts as success at war?

Enter Paul Yingling. In 2007, US Army Lieutenant Colonel Paul Yingling wrote perhaps the first truly viral essay of the military profession's digital era. Yingling ascribed America's lack of strategic success to a "failure in generalship"—that, as happened in Vietnam, "America's generals have been checked by a form of war that they did not prepare for and do not understand."[4]

Yingling wasn't alone. Steven Metz of the US Army War College piled on later with a dire warning: "It is time for Americans to think deeply about the skills their senior military leaders must have, otherwise we risk identifying those skills through the failures of military leaders who lack them."[5] Yet, unfortunately, Sarah Sewall, then of the Carr Center at Harvard University, also pointed out, "we lack the tools to judge military leadership."[6]

While they wear stars and camouflage to work, generals are just like the rest of us. They're people, and like the range of folks you engage with every day, they have their downs and ups.

There are some truly brilliant generals out there. The commander of all forces in South Korea when I served there was General Vincent Brooks. A tall, cerebral officer, he also happened to be a vegan and played basketball for Coach Mike Krzyzewski at West Point. Through the Modern War Institute at West Point I met retired General Stanley McChrystal, who commanded all forces in Afghanistan, and not long after, retired Admiral James Stavridis, the former Supreme Allied Commander Europe. As a sign of clear thinking and effective communication, both McChrystal and Stavridis went on to contribute insightful essays to book projects I organized.[7]

But then there was the retired three-star general who told another officer and me, "I paid some guy five hundred bucks to write my Command and General Staff College paper." We were in a military headquarters tent in South Korea in 2015. My colleague and I were majors then, and had just completed the same mid-career school the retired three-star mentioned in his confession. Without warning or prompting, this retired general point-blank bragged to us about his decades-past dishonorable bout of cheating.

While in that very same tent, over the very same period, we also worked for a one-star general with some serious issues. He would burst into manic fits that made him an agent of chaos. A wrecking ball with a big shiny star.

Once, during a field exercise, this general trapped a group of staff officers in a tent for hours to describe an operation he wanted us to plan. To "aid" our understanding, he scribbled on a blank sheet of paper until, over time, it became an incomprehensible black blob. A wide grin spread across the general's face as he handed his indecipherable page over to us as if it were the Single Strategy to Win All Wars. As a dark joke, we later posted it on a corkboard in our bunker headquarters and wrote "Plan B" under the swirly blob, with an addendum: "(pray for Plan A)."

So with generals, some are really good, some really bad, and some really ugly. The trick is to spot the difference.

Over time, grain by grain, little bits of gunpowder loaded the cartridge until my mind's starter pistol fired, triggering over a decade of research into generals, supreme commanders, and strategic leadership. I asked: What makes generals great, and what makes great generals? What accounts for successful supreme command at war?[8] Which strategic leaders make winning possible—and what might we learn from them?

These felt like such important questions because one context—generals at war—might unlock numerous lessons for so many other fields of strategic leadership.

Myths about leadership are everywhere. One mid-career military officer went a little overboard, writing, "True generalship is an ability to borrow elements of Patton's technical military competence and the moral pureness of Gandhi, mixed with Bill Clinton's artful communication, Ryan Crocker's diplomatic savvy, and George Kennan's strategic acumen—in other words, to approximate a fraction of the soul of George Marshall."[9]

That's a deity, not a general. It's too perfect, and perfection shouldn't pass anyone's poo-smell test.

Those in the military are often guilty of a subtler mythology—an unhealthy, myopic fixation on leadership.

Visiting West Point while still in service, I listened in rapid succession to the command sergeant major there say he wanted to build "leaders of character," the one-star commandant tell the cadets to "be a leader," and the three-star superintendent say he wanted West Point to be the "prime leader development institution in the world."

Leader-this, leader-that, lead, lead, lead. The military uses the word "leader" so much and so often that it's become an empty catchphrase.

It's not just those in uniform. Historian Jeremy Black, in a public lecture devoted to the question of how George Washington won the Revolutionary War, ultimately provided a one-word answer: "Leadership."[10]

Leadership is constant. At war—as in most competitions—both sides have leaders, and specifically, strategic leaders.

But when it comes to winning, leadership is not enough.

The better question: What differentiates successful strategic leadership from unsuccessful strategic leadership?

To answer this, I took on a dissertation and dug into the performance of three supreme commanders who steered wars to successful conclusions, over periods when the conflict might have gone a different way: George Washington in 1776 and into 1777, Ulysses S. Grant in

1864 through the presidential election that November, and Dwight D. Eisenhower in 1944 until the Allies took Paris and then France. Most importantly, I evaluated their performances in direct contrast with their adversaries', taking advantage of the "natural experiment" produced by their having fallen into "matched pairs."[11]

What made the difference?

It wasn't material factors, technology, weapons, or other stuff. It wasn't luck. Their adversaries were competent.

The difference was superior judgment and decision-making. The successful strategic leaders' judgments were objectively better than those of their unsuccessful adversaries.

Different military strategies. Different time periods. Different relative resources. Different war aims. All of these changed. Yet a careful reading of the dispatches and memorandums and decisions of the strategic leaders on both sides led me to conclude that a critical factor in each outcome was superior judgment.

Strategic leaders make decisions; decisions make history. Moreover, it seems that when it comes to strategy, it's not whether strategic leaders win or lose a given battle, but how they change the game. Washington surprised his adversary by unexpectedly choosing to fight on through the cold. Grant, in contrast to his predecessors, pushed his adversary into a continuous fight that ground the opposition down to nearly nothing. And Eisenhower's multiple landings along a broad front rolled the Nazis back to their home soil—which may not have been entirely surprising, yet his steady-handed steering nonetheless completed the European war's endgame.

The art of the general is the art of the better decision. Strategic leaders act as decision funnels composed of judgment, empathy, and grit, anchored by a sense of humble confidence. Ideas, opinions, options, and courses of action from all sources and places go in the top, but only one strategic choice comes out the spout below. This is in line with Sun Tzu's assertion in *The Art of War*—strategic leadership shapes and harnesses force like the power of water.[12]

The cases before these three generals were all big, pre-nuclear wars for the highest stakes. I make no one-size-fits-all claims here. However, Washington, Grant, and Eisenhower have something in common to teach us: Superior judgment matters.

If war is a gamble, they were the ones making the biggest bets.

And when we roll the iron dice, those bets count.

As a lieutenant who fought in Iraq, my first brush with war came as a scared, confused twenty-three-year-old. Ever since, I have struggled to understand why, and how, we fight. First as a dissertation—and now this book—this is my best effort at helping the next batch of scared, confused twenty-three-year-olds to understand their wars a little better.

If anyone needs a better breed of generals and admirals, or a sharper set of strategic leaders, it is them. On the deadly serious subject of who wins wars, we owe our future troops the best we can muster.

What follows is for them.

WHAT STRATEGIC LEADERS CAN SHOW US

A people unused to restraint must be led, they will not be drove.
—George Washington

Beaten, bloodied, and nearly broken, the Continental Army faced the "times that try men's souls," in the immortal words of Thomas Paine.[1] In early December 1776, the Army had just escaped New York into New Jersey, with only 3,000 soldiers remaining.[2] That December 7, they were only one hour ahead of an overwhelming British force in pursuit.[3] It seemed like the end. It probably should have been the end.

If America ever had a near-death experience, a brush with extinction, it was this moment.

So how did Lieutenant General George Washington manage to defeat the much stronger British army led by Lieutenant General William Howe?[4] The British had nearly every advantage—military force, economic might, and political will. Washington's army had to build everything from scratch while fighting one of the best-trained armies in the world.[5]

It's a battlefield success story for the ages with echoes all around us. David and Goliath, the underdog and the frontrunner. It's a common storyline readers should find familiar. But the gap between the two combatants isn't what's interesting in this case. What's interesting—even inspiring—is how Washington found a way to win despite the gap, because it begs a bigger question.

Who wins wars, and what can we learn from those who do?

It's such a crucial question to every one of us for at least two reasons.

First, it's at the core of how we secure all that we hold dear. Over three centuries, America has fought a war for survival, a war for unity, and a war for security. All were, to varying degrees, existential. We may yet fight for stakes as high in this century too.

So clearly we've got to find or build enough of the right strategic leaders to be ready for whatever comes next.

From the very week of America's birth, on July 2, 1776, George Washington's order to his troops addressed this exact need: "The fate of unborn Millions will now depend, under God, on the Courage and Conduct of this army."[6] Two hundred fifty years on, it still does. It still will. An army is connected to a people just as an arm is connected to a body. Each citizen must make wise decisions about the strategic leaders it selects to guide its army and arms.

Secondly—and thankfully—in most of the rest of our daily lives, the stakes of decision-making aren't nearly so high. But in some areas we certainly still need superior strategic leadership. In our schools. In our hospitals. In our cities. In our places of worship. In our small businesses. On our sidelines. Even when the stakes are far less than national survival, we need strategic leaders to step up and shine.

Because when it matters, it matters. And the opportunities are fewer than we realize.

★ ★ ★ ★

It is rare to get a second chance when lives are at stake, especially at war. Consider the Union, which got one under Ulysses S. Grant in May 1864.

Roughly one year prior, in May 1863, Union forces under Major General Joseph Hooker faced General Robert E. Lee's Army of Northern Virginia at the Battle of Chancellorsville. Hooker's Army of the Potomac outnumbered Lee's forces by better than a two-to-one margin (roughly 133,000 to 60,000). In the battle, Hooker sustained a little over 17,000 casualties; Lee just under 13,000.

At the time, military thinking went that you show up, you fight a battle, whichever side holds the field and inflicts more casualties is the winner, and everyone licks their wounds for several months until the next encounter. That's what Hooker did. He lost at Chancellorsville. Lee won. So Hooker backed away with his tail between his legs.

But not Grant. When he came up against the same circumstances that Hooker had, on almost exactly the same terrain, one year later, he changed the game. At the Battle of the Wilderness in May 1864, Grant's forces sustained roughly the same casualty figures as Hooker's one year prior. What differed was what came after. Instead of tucking tail, Grant instead took something else from tactical defeat. Sure, Lee inflicted damage. Yet the Union still had far more fighting strength in the field. And so Grant chose to continue to press, pushing the Confederates into a continuous fight that would, over time, grind them down until victory became inevitable.

That sort of second chance doesn't happen often. So when the time comes—like a patient hitter waiting for the right pitch—we can turn on a chosen fastball and knock it out of the park. Strategic opportunities are few and we've got to be prepared for each and every one. This book will help you sharpen that focus for these precious moments, on whichever field they come.

OUR ROADMAP

This book looks at how strategic leaders made decisions during war. It studies the big choices they faced, how they responded, and what happened after using focused, structured questions to detect patterns.[7] And a pattern did emerge: Each judgment first raised itself as a **challenge**; next, the leader made a **choice**; and last, there was a **clash** of forces, which led to **consequences**—and on to the next set of challenges, repeating the cycle. This is the cycle of strategic leadership.

What we too often do when considering strategic leaders is we jump straight to outcomes. But if we skip over the decisions that led to these outcomes, we miss what was at stake—along with each strategic leader's role in shaping history.

By focusing on each strategic leader's decision-making process, we can evaluate how superior or inferior that leader's choices were. We can also compare their thinking to see whose judgment was better. The goal is to understand what made a strategic leader more successful than their adversary.

I base all of this analysis on original documents—things like war reports and dispatches and memoranda and letters written at the time. These records show us how each commander thought through problems. As historian and British Major General J. F. C. Fuller once asked, what was "the governing reason for an action?"[8] This question helps us stay grounded in fact, since others at the time of these commanders' victories preferred different choices in the same situations. That means these strategic leaders had other real options.

War is more than just fighting—it's about outthinking your adversary.[9] Before any action comes thought. We can trace actions back to the thoughts behind them, thanks to these contemporary records.

Because military history gives us the best record of highest-stakes strategic competition, the book focuses on George Washington's campaign in 1776–1777, Ulysses S. Grant's efforts in 1864, and Dwight D. Eisenhower's invasion in 1944. We'll trace back from each war's successful end to the key campaign that had the biggest impact on the result. Some call this the "decisive" campaign, but we'll use the term "terminal" campaign—the moment when the war's ultimate conclusion was shaped the most.[10]

We'll set up the competitions as adversary on adversary, discuss each duel of decisions in depth, and then provide actionable takeaways and modern insights from today's strategic leaders while considering stories that illustrate where each great may have gone wrong—but instead made wise choices.

In this way, the book connects us with a far larger question: How can battlefield success lead to strategic victory? Put another way, how does what we do today lead to success tomorrow? For that, we can backtrack from a war-ending moment like the Confederate surrender at Appomattox Court House to a specific campaign like the Union's 1864 offensive (which we'll cover in the chapters on Grant). This campaign's outcome was tied to the war's end through what strategist Colin Gray calls "strategic effect"—the ability of one strategic leader to "generate desired effect upon the future course of events."[11] We'll travel that road and make that connection.

It helps to think about a two-person poker game where both players start with the same amount of money. In the end, one player has it all. That result is the objective final outcome—like a war's end. Yet, each individual hand was won against a subjective standard (the opponent's play). Both opponents played every hand based on their best understanding of the situation. Their goal was to win all the money, and the other player was the shifting standard against which they had to compete.

Working backward from a known, objective result, we can look for the moment when one player guaranteed their win. We then interrogate that moment to better understand how the cumulative, relative judgments—what to hold and when to fold—led to the loser's empty pockets. That moment helps us understand how one side's choices added up to success—or failure. This is why strategic leadership, to paraphrase Søren Kirkegaard, can only be understood backward (in hindsight).

Each of the strategic leaders we'll meet had plausible ways to achieve success.[12] Even the losing side must have had a path to victory when the terminal campaign began. To challenge the idea that the ultimate winners were destined to succeed—and to help avoid bias—this book also explores "what if" scenarios (counterfactuals) to explore how the losing sides might have won.[13] The reality is that at any given moment, there were roads not taken, and those untraveled roads give us a fuller picture of what happened and why.

For example, after being defeated at the Battle of Long Island, George Washington had to decide what to do: stay and fight on in New York, retreat, or even destroy the city so the British couldn't use it. He delayed for several days, listened to the advice of his top generals and the Continental Congress, and made a careful judgment: In the end, he chose to withdraw. That decision kept the army alive and avoided a possible trap in New York. By listening to both military and political advice, Washington managed to balance the interests of military leaders like Nathanael Greene, who wanted to burn the city, and political leaders like those in Congress, who preferred that he stay and defend New York. With multiple options supported by multiple stakeholders, Washington managed a wise decision.

It matters that there are credible historians who argue the terminal campaign's outcome might have gone another way. In short, the losing side could be said to have had "opportunity." Of course, this opportunity must include another quality: fighting power.

Martin van Creveld has written that fighting power includes all the physical, mental, and moral strength of an army.[14] It's not just about numbers or weapons, but whether a force has sufficient needs to reach its goals. As long as both sides have enough fighting power to win, strategic leadership becomes a deciding factor.

The truth is, most of the time we don't need a Washington, Grant, Eisenhower, or any other superior strategic leader. Moreover, the word "strategy" is often overused.

You can see it everywhere, it seems, up to and including the garbage truck that passed me on the road the other day (boldly proclaiming itself a part of "Strategic Waste Management"). Some will draw the conclusion that it is always necessary. That "strategy never sleeps" (the unfortunate tagline for a now-defunct publication). That strategy is always a factor and so must perpetually dominate our thoughts.

But it's just not so. If you're the New York Yankees and you play against some Little Leaguers, you don't need strategic leadership, because the raw materials you're gifted with are more than sufficient for the task at hand. The overmatch is enough.

Likewise, if you're an extra-experienced investor and you've got a group of entrepreneurs coming in for evaluation on a business proposal, you probably don't need all that much deep thought. Natural repetitions have probably given you all you need to spot a winner.

Or the stakes may not matter to you, as when you go gambling with friends on a social engagement. Or you simply don't care.

There's a sweet spot there. The endeavor must be competitive and/or complex, in a real, hostile environment, most often against some adversary. The endeavor also must be a true challenge or conflict. Something with real stakes. Something that matters to you.

If the environment isn't competitive or hostile—no need for superior strategic leadership.

If the stakes aren't high enough—no need for superior strategic leadership.

Think about how few moments in our lives actually fall into the intersection of those two categories. For most the list is very, very small—a handful, really, over the course of an entire lifetime. Most can count those on one hand, two at a stretch. Everything else is a little "blah." We don't need strategic leadership so much as applied common sense with a side of discipline.

So strategic leadership isn't always necessary.

But when it is, it really, *really* is. Which is what we're about to find out.

Part I

THE PURSUIT OF SUCCESS

Chapter 1

THE ONE STRATEGY THAT WORKS

No two wars are alike.
—Ulysses S. Grant

How many strategies are there?

In my course of studying successful strategic leaders, that question became more and more powerful over time. It came up because it helps us understand how many options both sides might have considered in a given fight.

Of course, military officer and historian Basil Liddell Hart argued we should always, always, go for the "indirect" approach. Another military officer–historian, Bob Bateman, said there are "three (and only three) types of military strategy."[1] Not to be outdone on volume, author Robert Greene's book insists there are 33 strategies of war, all of which can be applied to the "subtle social game of everyday life."[2]

Why can't we figure out precisely how many strategies are out there?[3]

Maybe it's because we like to classify. We like to name things. We love being the one who "discovers" something and then patents it to claim insight among peers. So we go around labeling and binning different strategies for different scenarios. For example, a "Fabian" strategy refuses to fight a superior force, so it's often "best used by the weaker force," according to Bateman. Or there's the well-known nuclear strategies like mutually assured destruction and massive retaliation. Or the nonviolent approaches waged by Gandhi and King to longer-term successes.

But these adjectives often merely describe the type of tactics employed in carrying strategies out. Typically these were the physical tactical implements, almost like a chef describing the menu she made as "knife-crafted" or "wok-centric."

So what's really the common denominator in strategies wielded by successful strategic leaders?

During research, I stumbled on William Ury's *Getting Past No*, the classic book on negotiating. Early on, Ury points out that "your single greatest opportunity as a negotiator is to *change the game*."

That's when it clicked. This is what these successful supreme commanders sought and achieved. For Washington, changing the game meant fighting on during the winter of 1776–1777, even after the British garrisoned their troops. Washington surprised his adversary by unexpectedly counterattacking in the cold. For Grant, changing the game meant embracing pain, knowing it would hurt the Confederates more in the long, brutal campaign slog of 1864. Unlike his predecessors, Grant pushed his adversary into a continuous fight that ground the opposition down to nearly nothing. For Eisenhower, changing the game meant focusing all Allied energies on the single most important objective in 1944. Eisenhower's decisions pushed the Nazis back to their own home soil and changed the war's endgame.

The second hint came from the screen. There's a scene in the second season of HBO's *Game of Thrones* when a main character (Tywin Lannister) sits in the charred ruins of a castle. He explains the castle was built to be impervious to invasion—that, once, it seemed the perfect defensible position.[4]

> *TYWIN LANNISTER: The tallest towers, the strongest walls. The Great Hall had thirty-five hearths. Thirty-five. Can you imagine? Look at it now. A blasted ruin. Do you know what happened?*
> *ARYA STARK: Dragons?*
> *TYWIN: Yes. Dragons happened. Harrenhal was built to withstand an attack from the land. A million men could have marched on these walls, and a million men would have been repelled. But an attack from the air with dragon fire? Harren and all his sons roasted alive within these walls. Aegon Targaryen changed the rules. That's why every child alive still knows his name.*

Something changed. Dragons. (In our world: airpower.) And when those dragons came along, they burned the supposedly impenetrable castle to a crisp. To cinders. To nothing. As an afterthought, Tywin remarks that their victory was about how they "changed the rules."

This is what strategy should be, what it must be, for strategic leaders. It's not seeking to win tomorrow or avoiding a loss today. Strategy's not about wins and losses in the near term, but how you change the game for the long run. Successful strategy is an earthquake that alters the ground in your favor. It's how you create a competitive edge that literally upends your opponent's ability or willingness to fight. That's what Washington, Grant, and Eisenhower made happen.

This is the only successful strategy. The one common feature. An asymmetric advantage for one side, a durable disadvantage to the other side. Of course this has infinite applications, but the common approach to sustained victory for strategic leaders is to change the game.

But why not just reach for the shelf and dust off a previously "branded" approach? Why not just grab for one of Greene's magical 33—like the "blitzkrieg strategy" or his "center-of-gravity strategy"—or, while we're at it, maybe let's contain China's rise just as containment once worked against the Soviets?

Because labels become limits. They straitjacket your strategy in shackles made decades before for a different adversary. As Grant put it, "Every war I knew anything about had made laws for itself, and early in our contest I was impressed with the idea that success with us would depend upon our taking advantage of new conditions. No two wars are alike, because they are generally fought at different periods, under different phases of civilization."[5]

Of course it's safe to use some shorthand to separate one approach from another. The problem is that far too often, we let the labels have far too much power.

Because, simple as it sounds, every competition is different. It's unhelpful—or even dangerous—to walk into the next challenge with a previous problem's solution (as when the United States marched a World War II mindset off to war in Vietnam, to disaster).

The successful wartime strategies of strategic leaders in close contests are bespoke, tailored, made to fit a certain war. Successful strategies aren't stratagems to be dusted off decades or centuries after previous use.

The adversaries, methods, environments, and objectives change, and so must the next strategy.

Today's strategic leaders blindly applying the approach of a Washington, a Grant, or an Eisenhower would look as foolish as if they pulled on a tricorn, slouch, or service cap worn in days of yore. It just wouldn't fit, physically or stylistically.

Same goes with other competitions. Strategic leadership is where game changers succeed.

What's the takeaway here?

It's that our obsession as practicing strategic leaders and strategists (and *Homo sapiens* are all practicing strategists, to be sure) should always be to change the game in which we want to succeed.

Depending on the arena, that change might look radically different. If at sports, you'll be bounded by a literal field of play, and maybe something akin to "marginal gains" might be a great approach, when every centimeter and fast-twitch fiber counts.

But in most other unbounded, open fields of competition, that's just not going to cut it. Let's say you figure out a way to pack 10% more bullets into every magazine of every gun you have on a battlefield. Great. But that doesn't much matter when the adversary hits you with the steel rain of artillery, or well-hidden explosives that take out tank tracks, or if they raid the supply depot holding all your food and water.

Or maybe say you build the world's best castle, with the highest, strongest walls and deepest, broadest moat.

It doesn't work because there's always another dragon.

The only question is whether that dragon is you.

Chapter 2

ON SUPERIOR STRATEGIC PERFORMANCE

*I do not believe in luck in war any more than luck in
business. Luck is a small matter, may affect a battle or
a movement, but not a campaign or a career.*
—Ulysses S. Grant

Strategic leadership doesn't accept "good" as good enough. (Just ask Lieutenant General William Howe, General Robert E. Lee, or Adolf Hitler.)

Let's take a step back. For the record, I liked Richard Rumelt's 2011 book, *Good Strategy/Bad Strategy: The Difference and Why It Matters*. It was insightful about the many flaws and faults common in strategy making. He precision-targeted several culprits.

Most strategy, in Rumelt's estimation, stems from "the active avoidance of the hard work of crafting a good strategy." When that happens, he writes, bad strategy arrives, in the form of "vague aspirations" and misses any attempt to "address critical issues."

In the book, Rumelt says he coined the term "bad strategy" at a US

Department of Defense Office of Net Assessment conference in 2007, which birthed his book's title.

Think about that for a moment. Is there some quantum of goodness the strategic leader is aiming for? Some level of "good" a strategic leader can aspire to? Or is there some badness "floor" a strategic leader has to step over to ensure they've escaped bad strategy?

Of course not.

There is no objective standard in strategic performance until it's all over. When in the fight, there is no obvious "good" or clear "bad." This isn't a grade-school math test. Strategic performance is subjective, because the adversary's efforts are the unknown standard we wage war against. That's why we can only evaluate strategic performance after the fact by looking at the sum total of what happened and taking both combatants into account.

Strategist and professor Colin Gray reinforced this principle. He once wrote that the strategist "need only be good enough" to succeed over an adversary.[1] Retired British Royal Navy officer Steven Jermy has also found that "the term 'good strategy' is a poor term. Strategy, generally speaking, is about a dialectic, it's about a confrontation, so that's why 'superior' is the much better term, because strategy can only be gauged in terms of confrontation."[2]

Gray once compared strategy to a bridge. The strategic leader's job is to connect overarching goals with daily actions—turning force into results. But the bridge isn't merely a finished product. Gray also asked, "Who holds the strategy bridge—and how do they hold it?"[3]

We're going to look closely at the moments when Washington, Grant, and Eisenhower built their "bridges"—and prevented their adversaries from doing the same. At these points, they made crucial decisions that connected military power to political outcomes. Studying these decisions shows how strategy is not just something you have, it's something you make. This is one way to understand strategy as a dynamic process, in addition to its role as a finished product.

We also know a strategic leader can do everything "right" in the strategy-making process and still lose at the real contest. Just because it looks great in the boardroom doesn't mean it will work on the battlefield.

Because the adversary's performance matters. The enemy votes, an act that makes strategic performance inherently subjective. A strategic leader should always aim to be superior to the adversary.

For example, in late 1776, British forces under Lieutenant General William Howe had an opportunity to end the Continental Army and potentially the Revolutionary War. Howe's judgment to halt his campaign in early December 1776[4]—when he had beaten Washington's forces down to a small fraction of the Continental Army's earlier strength—was poor in comparison to his opponent's choice.[5] Oppositely, Washington's decision to counterattack at Trenton and Princeton was superior, reversing Howe's gains and causing him to change plans for 1777. Washington also disrupted Howe's coordination with another British force, a mistake that later brought France into the war on the American side.

Another example, Lieutenant General Ulysses S. Grant's May–November 1864 campaign against General Robert E. Lee and the Confederates, was a simultaneous attack on all fronts that stripped away Lee's strength. Grant's emphasis on attrition included the denial of prisoner exchanges and support to enable Union soldiers in the field to vote in a presidential election with bearing on the battlefield. In contrast, Lee's offensive posture in Virginia, his desire to "take the initiative,"[6] was overaggressive (even allowing that Lieutenant General Jubal Early's raid was a useful deep strike on Washington, DC, at a pivotal moment). The net result was that Grant's superior judgment removed Lee's offensive capability, left Lee stuck in trenches surrounding Petersburg and Richmond, and assured President Abraham Lincoln another term in office.

Yet another example was General Dwight D. Eisenhower's preparation for and execution of the invasion of France, from March to August 1944, against the wartime supreme command of Adolf Hitler, loaded with decisions that blended tactical, operational, strategic, and political considerations. An issue that vexed Allied planners was how and where to employ airborne divisions to support D-Day's amphibious assault. Eisenhower's lead air planner, British Air Chief Marshall Trafford Leigh-Mallory, counseled that to drop the two airborne divisions where intended would result in "futile slaughter," likely costing "seventy per cent" of those men.[7]

Eisenhower overruled his subordinate's judgment, and this proved correct. The airborne drops, while imperfect, were militarily effective. Juxtapose those decisions with Hitler's mismanagement of the Atlantic Wall coastal fortification, for which he failed to make the crucial operational decision between a beach and mobile defense, leaving the Nazis "weak everywhere, strong nowhere."[8] As a result, by the end of the campaign, France was in Allied hands, Germany faced two opponents on its home borders, and the Allies were on the path to victory.

In each case—with Washington, Grant, and Eisenhower—superior strategic performance made a massive difference.

GRAY BEARDS AS GUIDES

At the height of the Iraq War, in late 2006, the *Los Angeles Times* asked a simple, powerful question: "How would four of the greatest war leaders in human history have handled Iraq?"

They asked Julius Caesar, Genghis Khan, George Washington, and Abraham Lincoln. None were available for comment.

Four eminent historians spoke for these giants. Adrian Goldsworthy was sure that Caesar would "win," but "how he would do it is harder to say."[9] Jack Weatherford noted that Genghis Khan's grandson Hulegu expanded the Mongol Empire by sacking Baghdad in 1258.[10] Their success was aided because the Mongols "immediately executed the caliph and his sons." Ruthless.

George Washington, according to Joseph J. Ellis, was an insurgent.[11] Washington grasped that "he did not have to win the war," and that "time and space were on his side." Tie goes to the insurgent. And historian Harold Holzer looked to Abraham Lincoln and advised that the two warring sides were well known to the other, as they are in many, if not all, civil wars.[12]

These were the historical experiences we were to consult to inform American strategic thinking on the Iraq War? Ellis even acknowledged a problem when he called it "ridiculous" to assert that George Washington could tell us much about Iraq.

Why?

It's been said that time is a river and no matter how hard you might try, you never step in the same river twice. Especially so far downstream, whether by two decades or two centuries or two millennia.

The consequence is that we can't look to history for specific answers. At best we can look for suggestions, tips, or nudges. Think of it this way. If time is a river, we'll never be able to pin down specific certain crossings, but we can identify, say, some stones likelier to be there to step on to get across, or even a section that should be shallower.

This isn't to say we should throw out our ancestors' accomplishments (or failings). Caesar, the Khans, Washington, and Lincoln all did big things that shaped our world. We can indeed learn something from them all, as we can from the great strategic leaders in this book.

And so while we're out Monday-morning-quarterbacking some of the greatest generals of all time—it's good to have guides along for the ride.

In the military, there's a nickname for the older, wisest members of the profession. We call them "gray beards." I hunted some down for this book.[13]

It's true that I've spent far more than a decade of my life studying Washington, Grant, and Eisenhower. It's true that I've served with and among generals and admirals of all ranks, right up to four stars. It's true that I've even collaborated with some of those senior military officers on projects. At times I've seen these minds in action. But I still thought it would be helpful to talk to some to better understand how this subject looks through their eyes, today, in our modern world. They can connect the decisions and experiences in our past to the decisions and experiences in our modern day. They can validate what's still useful and relevant.

These strategic leaders represent those "very real military minds" that—in otherwise awful circumstances—might have been called upon to take terrifying risks for the safety and security of the United States.[14]

So I recruited some truly outstanding gray beards. I found five of the sharpest retired senior officers from each of the four largest American military services.

From the Army: General (ret.) Austin Scott Miller is a former commander at all levels in the Special Operations community, was commander of Joint Special Operations Command, and served as the final commander of NATO's Resolute Support Mission in Afghanistan.

From the Navy: Rear Admiral (ret.) Mike Studeman served as director of the National Maritime Intelligence-Integration Office and commander of the Office of Naval Intelligence, as well as director of intelligence of US Indo-Pacific Command and for the US Southern Command.

From the Marine Corps: General (ret.) Robert Neller served as the Commandant of the Marine Corps, led the Third Marine Division and Marine Corps Forces Central Command, among others.

From the Air Force: General (ret.) Philip Breedlove served as the 17th Supreme Allied Commander Europe of NATO Allied Command Operations, and as commander of US European Command.

And Lieutenant General (ret.) Chris Miller served as Deputy Chief of Staff for Strategic Plans and Programs at Headquarters Air Force, was senior Air Force commander in Afghanistan, commanded America's only B-2 bomber wing, and was a distinguished graduate of the Air Force Academy, subsequently earning a master's degree as a Rhodes Scholar at Oxford University.

All were thoughtful, candid, and generous with their time in service of a simple idea—finding and building the next, better version of themselves. We spoke for an hour each on the subject of strategic leadership. How it's changed, where it's headed.

These gray beards had a lot to say—the total transcript topped 50,000 words, near as many as there are in this book. We're going to trot out several of their ideas along the way and aim to harness some of them—the ones they held in common, the ones that stood out.

They'll pop in and out when the opportunity presents itself, in discussing how Eisenhower won, how Grant won, and how Washington won.

Which is where our story starts.

Part II

HOW WASHINGTON WON

Chapter 3

CHALLENGE: WASHINGTON AND HOWE, 1776–1777

These are the times that try men's souls.
—Thomas Paine (December 1776)

I n 1776, the Continental Army faced disaster. British troops were much older and far more experienced—on average, 28 years old with seven years of military service. In contrast, American soldiers were about 20 years of age and had less than six months of training.[1] The British invasion force was enormous: 32,000 soldiers, 10,000 sailors, and 400 ships—larger than any American city at the time.[2] (Relative to today's national population, that would be an approximate invasion force of six million descending on New York City.) Washington had 16,000 troops in the area that month.[3]

The British were led by Lieutenant General William Howe. He and his top officers, major generals Henry Clinton and John Burgoyne, were among the best in the British army. Howe was chosen from 119 candidates, partly due to his impressive French and Indian War service.

Burgoyne said the war required a "genius of the first class," and many thought Howe was exactly that.[4]

Moreover, Howe's brother, Vice Admiral Richard Howe, led the British naval force. Their close relationship helped the army and navy work well together, especially for amphibious attacks along the coast.[5] Even Washington respected William Howe. On December 26, 1775, he wrote that Howe was "the most formidable enemy America has."[6]

It's not hard to see why historian and filmmaker Ken Burns recently assessed the American and Continental war effort and concluded it had "zero chance of working out . . . 250 years ago . . . the chances of the patriots prevailing are zero. And to tell the story of how it went from zero to one hundred percent is scary, violent, complicated, lots of undertow, and as exhilarating as you could possibly imagine."[7]

Washington became commander of the Continental Army on June 16, 1775, at 43 years old. Some thought highly of him; others considered him inexperienced.[8] He had managed a large estate in Virginia and fought for the British during the French and Indian War.[9] At just 22 years old, he went on a dangerous mission into the American frontier in 1754. He kept a detailed journal of the trip, which was later published and helped make his name known.[10]

Washington's background—his education, habits, personal traits, and experiences—all help explain how he made decisions and handled the heavy responsibilities of strategic leadership. One of his most important traits was a commitment to self-education. Throughout his life, Washington remained a serious writer. He wrote letters constantly, for political, military, and personal reasons. Historians agree that written communication was a major tool that Washington used to lead. In an age without phones or fast travel, Washington managed a newly formed national army through his words, written and delivered across great distances.[11]

Though he had little formal schooling by modern standards, he became one of the most widely read and well-informed men of his time. Washington was also one of the wealthiest individuals in colonial America, and he used some of that wealth to build an extensive and diverse personal library. The books he owned show how curious and serious he was about learning.[12]

At the time of his death, his library included works on nearly every major subject. If we're all the sum total of our chosen inputs, then Washington chose wisely. A sample of what was in his personal library:

An encyclopedia, books on taxation, farming, gardening, and horse care; *The History of the Decline and Fall of the Roman Empire* by Edward Gibbon; poetry collections; *Natural History* by Georges Louis Leclerc Buffon; histories of Spain, Ireland, and Louisiana; Shakespeare's plays; *Don Quixote*; a book on projectiles; Walter Minto's *Theory of Planets*; *Gulliver's Travels* by Jonathan Swift; arithmetic textbooks; the Bible; a guide to architecture; books on Native American tribes, commerce, criminal law, domestic law, geography, and atlases; works on the philosophy of Seneca; and many volumes on agriculture.[13]

Washington was also well read in military matters. His collection included:

a book on French Marshal Maurice de Saxe's reforms to the French army, a volume on national defense, writings on the

French Revolution, *An Essay on the Art of War* by Count Turpin (translated by Captain Joseph Otway), Walter Harte's biography of King Gustavus Adolphus of Sweden, John Muller's book on fortifications, essays on artillery by John Anderson, and a treatise on military discipline.[14]

Interestingly, Washington also collected books and writings about his British opponents. Among these were *The American Rebellion: Sir Henry Clinton's Narrative of His Campaigns, 1775–1782*, a book on King George III's reign, and items titled "List of Military Officers British & Irish in 1777," "Advice of Officers of the British Army," and "List of Officers Under Sr. Wm. Howe in America."[15] These books and lists suggest that Washington tried to understand his adversaries' mindset, strategy, and organization. And perhaps this understanding led him to avoid demonizing them (it's hard to think straight when you're full of hate). It's a useful lesson, that as personally awful as one might find enemy behavior, a strategic leader must always seek to anticipate the adversary's next move.

All this points to a man deeply invested in learning.[16] His reading covered science, politics, history, philosophy, and warfare. This broad education helped him think clearly and make informed decisions. It also reveals something important about his character. Washington didn't rely only on others to tell him what to think—he worked hard to teach himself. This independence of mind was likely a powerful source of strength in finding ways to be a battlefield game changer.

His esteem for education lasted his whole life. In the last political letter he wrote before he died, Washington argued that the United States needed a national military academy. He believed such a school was "of primary importance to this country."[17] That letter showed he was thinking not only about the present but also about building a better future for the nation (and that discussion subsequently led to the establishment of the United States Military Academy at West Point).

The war's geography was a challenge for both sides. Roads were few and rough, rivers mostly unbridged, and major cities all coastal. As retired general and historian Dave Palmer noted, perhaps the most important geographic feature was how sparsely populated the colonies were.[18] Philadelphia was the British Empire's second-largest city after London. Only three other cities—Boston, New York, and Charleston—had over 10,000 people. The colonies' total population of 2.5 million was spread across 1,100 miles.[19] Fighting a war across such a wide area, with so few roads, was a challenge to both sides. But British sea power provided superior coastal mobility.

On October 26, 1775, after the earlier battles of Lexington and Bunker Hill, King George III spoke in Parliament about the war:

> The rebellious war . . . is manifestly carried on for the purpose of establishing an independent empire. I need not dwell upon the fatal effects of the success of such a plan. The object is too important, the spirit of the British nation too high, the resources with which God hath blessed her too numerous, to give up so many colonies which she has planted with great industry, nursed with great tenderness, encouraged with many commercial advantages, and protected and defended at much expense of blood and treasure.[20]

King George III believed it wise "to put a speedy end" to the conflict by increasing his military forces in the colonies. When the rebels recognized their mistake, he said, "I shall be ready to receive the misled with tenderness and mercy." He offered a promise to authorize "certain persons" to grant pardons "upon the spot" in America.[21]

Lord George Germain, the British minister in charge of the war, agreed that a quick, "decisive blow" was needed.[22] Britain wanted to pressure the colonists into giving up and returning to their old relationship with London.[23] But how much pressure would be enough?

The British considered several strategies. One was a blockade, but Vice Admiral Howe said that was too big a task, even for the world's strongest navy. Another was terror, a method used in Scotland and Ireland, but Lieutenant General Howe found the terror approach dishonorable and unlikely to work. A third option, pushed by Major General Clinton, was to chase the Continental Army and destroy it completely. But Howe thought this would waste resources and might only bring short-term tactical wins. Another idea was the "ink-blot" strategy—taking small areas and slowly expanding control—but that would likely take too long.[24]

The best plan, Howe thought, was to control key river routes, especially the Hudson River. Doing so would cut New England off from the rest of the colonies and limit rebel movement, allowing Britain to defeat the Continental Army unit by unit.[25] Howe also believed most Americans were loyal to Britain and that winning their support would make a big difference. He wrote that "the insurgents are very few, in comparison of the whole people."[26]

On April 23, 1776, Lieutenant General Howe wrote to Lord Germain to lay out his strategic vision for the campaign: "the army . . . by rapid movements [will] bring the rebels to an action upon equal terms, before they could cover themselves by works of any significance." Howe desired a rapid, overwhelming strike in order to gain the "decisive action" he wanted.[27] His biggest fear was that the Americans would avoid direct fighting and stretch the war out.[28] Lord Germain agreed; he also sought "to finish the rebellion in one campaign."[29] Two days later, Howe wrote again, saying New York would be his main goal. He also wanted to act quickly before the spirit of rebellion spread too far after the British evacuation of Boston in the spring of 1776.[30]

In January 1776, Howe estimated he needed 20,000 troops.[31] He got far more—32,000 soldiers and 10,000 sailors by that summer.[32] On June 8, 1776, he thanked Germain for his "masterly" support.[33] Howe had everything he assessed he'd need to win that year.

By contrast, the American goal was simpler: survival. Easier than trying to conquer and control a distant country.[34] The Americans thought through several strategies. One was privateering—using ships to attack British trade—but that wouldn't do enough damage. Another, suggested by Major General Horatio Gates, was a long westward retreat into the interior to wear out the British, but that would leave civilians in cities unprotected. Major General Charles Lee favored using small independent fighting units, but they lacked power to defeat larger British units. For a moment, Washington supported a "war of posts," using strong defensive positions to avoid open battle. A variation of this was the "offensive-defensive," with limited offensive attacks supported by a wider defensive strategy. One appealing but impossible idea was to defend everywhere—militarily unrealistic but politically popular.

In the end, Washington used parts of all these strategies at different times, adjusting each to fit new situations.[35] He stayed flexible, and focused on survival to keep the cause alive.

COULD THE BRITISH HAVE WON EITHER
THIS CAMPAIGN OR THE WAR?

Was the American victory guaranteed? Could Lieutenant General Howe have won the 1776 campaign? Could the British have won the war?

Historians agree that the outcome was not inevitable. Experts like Piers Mackesy, James Scudieri, and Jeremy Black agreed the British had a real chance to win.[36] Their best opportunity for victory came in the latter part of 1776, when their army was strongest and the Continental Army was at its weakest.[37]

Historian Dave Palmer has pointed out that the war could have ended in many different ways:

> Perhaps Britain would have held onto portions of the provinces. Maybe rebel diehards . . . would have carved out a redoubt in the forest vastness beyond the Appalachians . . . at several points in the struggle they should have expected to achieve far less than [the Americans] eventually did.[38]

The war didn't have to turn out the way it did. The Americans might have lost.

Many historians believe that from 1776 to early 1777, the odds favored the British.[39] And British generals like Howe were not fools or cowards.[40] They were smart and skilled leaders.

Even the Americans fighting the war were unsure they would win. One of Washington's top generals, Major General Nathanael Greene, wrote to John Adams on June 2, 1776, that the outcome of the war was "very uncertain."[41]

Washington himself doubted success many times. In January 1776, he wrote to his aide, Lieutenant Colonel Joseph Reed:

The reflection upon my Situation, & that of this Army, produces many an uneasy hour when all around me are wrapped in Sleep. Few People know the Predicament we are In, on a thousand Accts.[42]

Later, on September 30, 1776, Washington wrote about how difficult the situation was:

"Such is my situation that if I were to wish the bitterest curse to an enemy on this side of the grave, I should put him in stead with my feelings."[43]

And on December 17, 1776, days before launching his bold surprise attack on Trenton, he wrote to his cousin and estate manager to "have my Papers in such a Situation as to remove at a short notice," so unsure was Washington of the attack's outcome.[44]

The revolution's leadership wasn't confident in victory. They were worried and under great pressure. This was the mood and mindset of the Continental Army, and George Washington himself, as the campaign began in the summer of 1776.

Chapter 4

CHOICES AND CLASHES: WASHINGTON AND HOWE, 1776–1777

On every side there is a choice of difficulties.
—George Washington (September 8, 1776)

SHOULD WASHINGTON DEFEND NEW YORK? SHOULD HOWE ATTACK ARMIES OR CITIES?

There was no single moment that decided the war, but by studying these choices—especially in adversarial pairs—we can learn what separates a successful strategic leader from one who fails. We can also understand how Washington and Howe thought about these key judgments.

In the spring of 1776, much of the Continental Army was already in New York. The colonies hadn't yet declared independence, but the fear of a British attack on the city pushed leaders toward a formal announcement of independence.[1] John Adams called New York the link between the northern and southern colonies and said it was key to the whole continent.[2] Both Washington and the Continental Congress agreed it should be defended.

Washington sent Major General Charles Lee ahead to prepare the city's defenses. Lee's early assessment letter to Washington on February 19, 1776, admitted, "What to do with the City, I own puzzles me, it is so encircle'd with deep navigable water, that whoever commands the Sea must command the Town."[3] Ten days later, Lee wrote again, explaining how difficult it was to build defenses and fortifications, since the geography made it easy for ships to attack.[4]

Even with this problem, there was never a serious discussion about abandoning New York. When Washington went to a strategy meeting with Congress in late May 1776, defending the city was considered so necessary it wasn't even mentioned.[5]

Then the British arrived. According to historian Andrew Jackson O'Shaughnessy, the British invasion force that landed on June 29 and July 12, 1776, was the largest ever sent across the Atlantic Ocean. Two-thirds of the British army and nearly half its navy were in America and the Caribbean. About 400 ships were in or around New York. In total, more than 42,000 British and Hessian (German) troops arrived.[6]

Washington's choice to defend the city was about more than just military strategy—it was also about politics. His 16,000 troops were dispersed in five positions: three on Manhattan Island, one at the far northern tip of Manhattan at Fort Washington, and one across the river in Brooklyn and Long Island.[7] Washington hoped the defenses might wear down the British or give the Americans a major win that would boost morale and political support.[8]

On July 2, 1776, Washington gave powerful orders to his troops:

> The fate of unborn Millions will now depend, under God, on the Courage and Conduct of this army . . . We have therefore to resolve to conquer or die . . . The Eyes of all our Countrymen are

now upon us . . . Let us therefore animate and encourage each other, and shew the whole world, that a Freeman contending for Liberty on his own ground is superior to any slavish mercenary on earth.[9]

A week later, on July 9, he received the Declaration of Independence from Congress and ordered it to be read aloud to all the troops.[10] Just as the British military threat arrived, the American political movement had simultaneously matured into a formal rebellion. On July 10, Washington wrote to Congress that he felt hopeful. If his troops fought bravely, the British would have to go through terrible bloodshed to win.[11]

Still, Washington didn't just sit and wait. On July 12, he called a meeting of his generals to ask whether they should launch a surprise attack on the British camped on Staten Island. All voted no.[12] On August 12, Washington admitted in a letter to John Hancock that he had no new information, but did not retreat.[13]

Then, on August 27, the British attacked, winning the Battle of Long Island. It was the biggest battle ever fought in North America to that time. The British lost about 350 soldiers, mostly wounded—while the Americans lost around 300 killed and over 1,000 captured (including three generals).[14]

Lieutenant General William Howe's choice at this moment was whether to focus on destroying the Continental Army or key locations.[15] This issue came up clearly in his New York campaign.

To Howe, New York was important because many in the city still supported the British. His naval advantage meant it would be easier to control than other places. He also believed the war would end only through some kind of political settlement. That meant he didn't want to destroy Washington's army. Instead, he wanted to beat them just enough to encourage surrender. His goal became taking cities like New York rather than destroying the rebel army.[16]

This led to disagreements between Howe and his second-in-command, Major General Henry Clinton. Clinton wanted to destroy Washington's army, but Howe didn't believe that was realistic. Howe deliberately chose not to push hard against the Continental Army in pursuit after routing the Americans on Long Island.[17]

Following Long Island, there remained the issue of retreating American troops. Nine thousand Continental troops under Washington sought to evacuate back across the river to rejoin the rest of the force, aided by some fog that helped conceal the withdrawal.

British naval officer Captain George Collier, who commanded a warship in New York harbor at the time of the Battle of Long Island, later wrote that he had expected to be ordered into the East River to block those Americans from escaping Long Island. He wrote that if just one ship had been placed there, not a single American soldier would have gotten away. Because this didn't happen, Collier said, the war was now to drag on much longer.[18]

He wasn't alone. British officer Charles Stedman also said that the Americans could have been trapped and forced to surrender. He said it would have been a "decisive victory" to trap the rest of the Continental Army force on Long Island.[19] According to Stedman—as with Collier—all it would have taken was one armed ship in the river to block the escape.

Howe's cautious approach was criticized right away. American Major General Israel Putnam said, "General Howe is either our friend or no general . . . [Howe] had our whole army in his power . . . Had he instantly followed up his victory [at Long Island] the consequences to the cause of liberty must have been dreadful."[20]

Clinton later wrote about three instances in this period when he told Howe to attack and was ignored.[21] One of those was after the Battle of Long Island. Clinton proposed landing troops north of Manhattan at a place called Spuyten Duyvil.[22] That would have blocked Washington's later escape by controlling a key bridge. Clinton argued this would have stopped the rebels from getting away when the British moved on Manhattan Island. But Howe told Clinton he didn't want to move until the rest of his supplies and troops arrived, including the Hessians.

Later, after the British took Fort Washington on the northern part of Manhattan Island in mid-November 1776, Clinton was given new orders. He was sent to lead a campaign to take Rhode Island.[23] This was surprising because the Continental Army was at its weakest, with fewer than 3,000 soldiers left.[24] Clinton wanted to strike Washington while his forces were extremely vulnerable, but Howe chose differently. Clinton later said he never supported that idea. He believed it was only done because the navy wanted a better winter base—a lesser objective in Clinton's view. Still, on November 26, 1776, Clinton left New York to capture Newport, Rhode Island.[25]

Though there's no single smoking gun explaining why Howe held back from more aggressive action, his own testimony in 1779 on his actions at this time of the war shows he was cautious. He believed that his "most essential duty" was to carefully commit his troops because a loss by his army "could not speedily, nor easily, be repaired."[26] He also wrote to Lord Germain that it would be hard to force the Americans into a major battle. The rebels controlled the interior, and the farther in they were from the coast and water, the more difficult it was for the British to reach them.[27]

SHOULD WASHINGTON WITHDRAW FROM NEW YORK? HOW SHOULD HOWE OFFER PARDONS?

The loss at Long Island forced Washington to call a Council of War on August 29, 1776. At the meeting, he asked his officers if they should "leave Long Island [and Brooklyn]" and move the Continental Army to New York (modern-day Manhattan). All agreed.[28]

But even after moving to Manhattan, Washington still had to decide whether to hold New York City at all. On September 2, 1776, he wrote to John Hancock, president of the Continental Congress:

> Our situation is truly distressing . . . The Militia . . . almost by whole Regiments and by Companies at a time are running away when fronted by a well appointed Enemy, superior in number to our whole collected force . . . I am obliged to confess my want of confidence in the Generality of the Troops . . .
>
> It is painfull and extremely grating to me to give such unfavourable accounts, but It would be criminal to conceal the truth at so critical a juncture . . . If we should be obliged to abandon this Town, ought It to stand as Winter Quarters for the Enemy? They would derive great conveniences from It on the one hand—and much property would be destroyed on the other—It is an important question, but will admit of but little time for deliberation.[29]

In this letter, Washington explained the challenge clearly. First, he said that many militia soldiers were running from the enemy and fleeing the battlefield. Second, he explained how hard it would be to defend New York. And third, he told Congress that they might lose the city—and asked if they should destroy it to keep the British from using it. He left that final decision to Congress, showing his respect for civilian leadership.

The next day, on September 3, Hancock replied that Congress had decided "that no Damage should be done to the City of New York."[30] Congress didn't want to be seen as burning one of the colonies' great cities. But the letter didn't say anything about whether Washington should keep troops in the city or pull them out.

A few days later, on September 5, 1776, Major General Nathanael Greene wrote a long, detailed letter to Washington about this very issue. In it Greene pointed to an ugly truth: To defend New York would jeopardize the entire army.[31] He made a strong case for retreating—and even burning the city. He argued this would protect the army and weaken the enemy.[32] But he only reflected on the military side of the issue. He didn't have to answer to Congress or consider political consequences the way Washington did.

Washington faced a tough decision. Greene's military advice was to leave and possibly burn the city. Congress had said not to burn it. Washington had to think about more than just winning battles—he had to keep the army together and maintain support from the people and Congress. If he burned New York, would the people of other cities—like Philadelphia—worry they might be next? Would they then turn against the revolution?

To work through the issue, Washington called another Council of War on September 7, 1776. He reported the results to Hancock in a letter the next day:

It is now extremely obvious from all Intelligence . . . they mean to inclose us on the Island of New York . . . Having therefore their

System unfolded to us, It became an important consideration how It could be most successfully opposed—On every side there is a choice of difficulties . . .

. . . on our side the War should be defensive, It has been even called a War of posts, that we should on all occasions avoid a general Action . . . With these views & being fully persuaded that It would be presumption to draw out our young Troops into open Ground against their superiors both in number and discipline, I have never spared the Spade & Pickax.[33]

Here, Washington said he believed the British wanted to trap the Continental Army in New York. He also admitted that his soldiers were not ready to face the British in a direct fight. But he also explained that even staying on defense in New York wouldn't work:

The honour of making a brave defence does not seem to be a sufficient stimulus when the success is very doubtfull . . . We are now in a strong post but not an Impregnable one.[34]

Washington walked a fine line. He didn't want to abandon the city without a fight, but he also didn't want to risk the entire army. So he chose a middle path. He moved some supplies and troops out of the city while keeping the rest in place:

I have also removed from the City All the Stores & Ammunition except what was absolutely necessary for Its defence . . . It was concluded to Arrange the Army under Three Divisions, 5000 to remain for the defence of the City, 9000 to Kingsbridge . . . The remainder to occupy the intermediate space . . .[35]

In the same letter, he described the argument made by officers like Greene who wanted to abandon the city completely:

There were some Genl Officers . . . that were for a total and immediate removal . . . urging the great danger of One part of the Army being cut off . . . That by removing from hence we deprive the Enemy of the Advantage of their Ships . . . But they were overruled by a Majority.[36]

Washington shared both sides of the argument. But in closing, he hinted at his personal view:

I am sensible a retreating Army is encircled with difficulties, that the declining an Engagement subjects a General to reproach and that the Common cause may be affected by the discouragement It may throw over the minds of many. Nor am I insensible of the contrary Effects if a brilliant stroke could be made . . . But when the Fate of America may be at Stake . . . we should protract the War.[37]

He made it clear that he expected to leave the city eventually. The goal was to do so without risking the whole army.

Then, on September 11, 1776, Washington's generals met once more. This time, they voted to overturn their earlier decision and evacuate the city. Washington wrote to Hancock on September 14:

I could wish to maintain It, Because I know It to be of Importance, But I am fully convinced that It cannot be done . . . a large Majority . . . determined a removal of the Army prudent but absolutely necessary.[38]

In less than one week, from September 8 to September 14, Washington changed his mind. First he tried to hold part of the city. But in the end, he agreed full withdrawal was the only option. He even left behind a few men to stay back to spy on the British, including a young officer named Nathan Hale. Hale pretended to be a schoolteacher to gather intelligence but was quickly caught. The British hung Hale on September 24 without trial.[39] This showed how fast the British took control of the city.

By the end of September 1776, even though Washington received some reinforcements, he had fewer than 15,000 troops fit for duty. Howe still had far over 40,000.[40] Washington's decision to pull back gave him time to fight another day.

The British believed the heart of the American rebellion was in Massachusetts.[41] But instead of focusing there, they turned their attention to New York and offered pardons as a way to end the war. These efforts matched the views of British Major General James Robertson, who said, "I never had the idea of subduing the Americans, I meant to assist the good Americans to subdue the bad ones."[42] The British strategy was based on the belief that many colonists were loyal and just needed help defeating the rebels. William Howe agreed. He wrote that loyalists were "very few, in comparison of the whole people," suggesting he believed most Americans would eventually return to British rule if given the right terms.[43]

The Howe brothers were given some authority to negotiate peace. On June 22, 1776, Vice Admiral Howe received the king's instructions and passed them along to his brother.[44] However, there was disagreement in London over how much power the Howes should have. Vice

Admiral Howe wanted wide freedom to offer pardons and concessions. But Lord George Germain, who oversaw American affairs, disagreed. He insisted on granting pardons only to those who swore loyalty to the King. Germain even said he would resign rather than grant the Howes more control.[45]

Two moments show how serious Lieutenant General Howe was about using pardons. The first was on July 13, 1776, not long after the British arrived in New York. The British tried to contact George Washington, but refused to call him "General." Instead, they addressed their letter to "Mister Washington" or "Geo. Washington etc. etc. etc." This was a problem because calling him "General" would have meant publicly acknowledging him as a legitimate military leader, not a traitor.[46] So Washington rejected the letter. Accepting it would have been an admission that the Continental Army was not part of a legitimate separate government.

Washington explained his decision in a letter to Congress:

I would not upon any occasion sacrifice Essentials to Punctilio [protocol], but in this Instance, the Opinion of Others concurring with my own, I deemed It a duty to my Country and my appointment to insist upon that respect which in any other than a public view I would willingly have waived.[47]

The two sides met briefly in rowboats, but since the British refused to recognize Washington, no conversation happened. Germain's orders didn't allow any real talks unless the Americans surrendered first.[48] This condition rendered negotiations impossible.

Meanwhile, the British command still hoped that American forces would break. On September 3, 1776, after the British won the Battle of

Long Island, Henry Strachey—a secretary to both Howe brothers—wrote a letter describing this hope:

> As their Regiments are from almost every Province on the Continent, it is probable that many of them may begin to look towards their respective homes, and contend for the Recovery of those Liberties which have been most grievously invaded by the Tyranny of their own Countrymen, under the Pretext of preserving them from the imaginary Apprehensions of ours.
>
> Of New Jersey . . . we know little . . . but as we are so near them, and the superiority of the King's Forces is now beyond a doubt with them.[49]

Strachey believed that once the Americans started losing on the battlefield, they would turn against their own leaders and come back to British rule. Given this hope, it made sense that Lieutenant General Howe emphasized pardons.

On September 11, 1776, the only formal meeting between American and British leaders during the campaign took place.[50] It didn't go anywhere. The Declaration of Independence, recently signed, blocked serious talks. King George III didn't recognize the Declaration, and so Britain wouldn't treat the Americans as equal negotiation partners.

The American team—Benjamin Franklin, John Adams, and John Rutledge—met with Vice Admiral Howe.[51] Still, the British position hadn't changed. The King would only pardon those "subjects . . . as shall deserve our Royal Mercy." Since the Declaration made all Americans rebels, the pardon couldn't apply to anyone in opposition to British rule.[52]

Lieutenant General Howe hoped the American loss at Long Island would make the Continentals more willing to negotiate.[53] But even

Strachey doubted that would happen. He wrote on September 3, "[The Americans] might at this moment have peace and happiness, but they insist upon having their brains knocked out first."[54]

Strachey was partly right. Even though Washington had to retreat from New York, the Americans did not give up. On September 25, 1776, Lieutenant General Howe admitted in a report, "I found the Americans not so well disposed to join us, and to serve us as I had been taught to expect; that I thought our farther progress for the present, precarious."[55]

Still, the British tried again. On November 30, 1776, Vice Admiral Howe issued a new offer: Any American who swore loyalty to King George III within sixty days would be pardoned.[56] By late December, the offer seemed to be gaining support. In a letter to his wife on December 28, Henry Strachey wrote, "The Proclamation of the 30th. Of last Month has reformed a Croud of Culprits, and I cannot deliver out of the King's Pardons so fast as they are claimed."[57]

About 5,000 Americans signed the pardon oath. But this did not last. When Washington later won surprise victories at Trenton and Princeton, most who had signed the oaths rejected them. Morale shifted back in favor of the revolution. After those victories, Strachey concluded that the Americans "still continue obstinate."[58]

SHOULD HOWE CULMINATE THE CAMPAIGN? SHOULD WASHINGTON ATTACK?

In the latter part of 1776, Lieutenant General William Howe won important victories at White Plains and Fort Washington, both located on the far north end of modern-day New York City. These battles pushed Washington and the Continental Army out of New York and into New

Jersey. At White Plains, Howe claimed success and forced the Americans to speed their retreat. Later, in a personal statement, he explained his decision not to attack further:

> The committee must give me credit when I assure them, that I have political reasons, and no other, for declining to explain why that assault was not made . . . . If, however, the assault had been made, and the lines carried, the enemy would have got off without much loss . . . By forcing the lines we should undoubtedly have gained a more brilliant advantage, some baggage, and some provisions; but we had no reason to suppose that the rebel army could have been destroyed.[59]

Howe believed attacking wasn't worth the cost in soldiers and would not have gained much. Instead, he tried to outmaneuver Washington, pushing him without taking big risks. This cautious approach worked in the short term. When the British captured Fort Washington on November 16, 1776, they took over 2,800 American soldiers prisoner.[60] Even worse, Washington had to watch from across the Hudson River at Fort Lee as many of his men were killed—some stabbed with bayonets or beaten to death.[61] Washington was so distraught that he reportedly turned and cried.[62]

By mid-December, with the Continental Army in retreat, Howe believed the campaign was over. He stopped the chase and spread his forces across New Jersey, New York City, and Newport, Rhode Island, for the winter.[63] His second-in-command, General Henry Clinton, disagreed strongly. Clinton later wrote:

> [U]pon [Howe's] hinting to me his intention of running a chain of posts across east Jersey, I took the liberty of cautioning him

against the possibility of its being broken in upon in the winter . . . I even advised him, after having pushed Washington to the utmost, if he could not succeed in taking his army, to evacuate the Jersies altogether.[64]

This account came after the war—with hindsight—so we should view it with caution. However, Howe's own testimony supports the idea that Clinton had warned him. Howe later defended his choices this way:

But it has been objected to me that I ought not to have intrusted the important port of Trenton to the Hessian troops. My answer to this . . . Military men will certainly understand it. The left, Sir, was the post of the Hessians in the line, and had I changed it upon this occasion it must have been considered a disgrace . . . And it probably would have created jealousies between the Hessian and British troops, which it was my duty carefully to prevent.

My principal object in so great an extension of the cantonments was to afford protection to the inhabitants . . . that they might experience the difference between his majesty's government, and that to which they were subject from the rebel leaders.[65]

Howe's reasoning was consistent. He wanted to keep good relations between his British and Hessian troops and to win over local civilians by showing them the benefits of British rule. He thought this approach would turn more Americans back toward loyalty. But his choice left his forces vulnerable.

On December 1, 1776, Lieutenant James Monroe (later the fifth US president) counted Washington's army and reported that it had fallen to only 3,000 men.[66] The Continental Army was moving south out of Newark, trying to escape. At one point, British forces were just one hour behind Washington's troops, which arrived in Princeton on the afternoon of December 7.[67]

The next day, December 8, the Americans reached and crossed the Delaware River into Pennsylvania. Instead of continuing chase, Howe halted pursuit. On December 13, 1776, he issued orders for his troops to go into winter quarters. He personally selected the towns where his soldiers would stay, placing three brigades about six miles apart so they could forage more freely for food and still provide mutual support. He placed Colonel Johann Rall and his Hessian troops in Trenton—the closest to Washington's forces. Howe judged the fighting was done until spring.[68]

Not everyone in the British military agreed with Howe's judgment. Charles Stedman, a British officer at the time, criticized the plan. He wrote that the line of British posts from the Delaware River to Hackensack was "too extensive," and that the garrisons were "too remote from each other." He added, "Foreign troops ought not to have been stationed either at Trenton or Bordenton" as "they lay nearest to the enemy." The Hessians "were unable to obtain proper intelligence, and instead of conciliating the affections, made themselves particularly disagreeable to the natives, by pillaging them."[69]

British Major General James Robertson echoed this complaint. He reported that after being robbed by soldiers, many in New Jersey "took up their weapons and began to fight back."[70]

Stedman gave a scathing summary of Howe's decision-making: "Men of plain sense could not understand why," with such a powerful and experienced Army, Howe "should suffer an undisciplined army, not amounting to a sixth part of his own numbers."[71]

So, while Howe believed he was acting reasonably, his decision to halt the campaign—and his failure to destroy Washington's army when he had the chance—proved costly.

The numbers make the mistake clearer. On August 27, 1776, at its maximum in the campaign, the Continental Army had around 19,000 effective soldiers. By November 28, only about 3,000 remained.[72] Upon landing in the colonies, the British had about 32,000 ground troops (excluding sailors at sea). Even after garrisoning captured towns, the British had around 14,000 soldiers near New Jersey in early January 1777 (the closest in time a credible comparison seems available).[73]

Despite such a favorable advantage, Howe allowed the Americans to escape, which is when things changed drastically. On December 7, 1776, British forces were one hour behind Washington's army. By not pressing the attack, Howe gave Washington time to regroup. The Americans gained reinforcements—mostly militia—and their numbers grew from 3,000 to 6,500 in late December 1776. By early January 1777, Washington had 7,500 soldiers.[74]

From November to early December 1776, Howe had a better than four-to-one advantage over Washington. By early January, that advantage shrunk to about two-and-a-half-to-one. Even worse, Howe split his forces into smaller, isolated garrisons. This provided Washington his opportunity to strike.

This stretch—from late November to early December—was the period of greatest danger for the Continental Army and all of America. Had Howe acted more aggressively, he might have ended the war. But by deciding to pause the campaign, and by spreading out his forces in vulnerable positions, Howe gave Washington the opportunity to recover and hit back.

On September 30, 1776, General George Washington wrote a letter to his cousin and estate manager, Lund Washington, in which he expressed his deep despair. He confessed, "In confidence I tell you that I never was in such an unhappy, divided state since I was born."[75]

This was a rough stretch for him, as the situation around his army looked worse by the day.

Washington often brought his officers together for war councils to discuss major decisions. One of these meetings occurred shortly after the American defeat at the Battle of White Plains on November 6, 1776. At this council, the leaders "unanimously agreed" to "throw a Body of Troops into the Jerseys immediately."[76]

Around this time, Washington wrote to his brother, John Augustine Washington. He started the letter on November 6, 1776, and continued writing on November 19. In the first part, Washington reflected on the loss at White Plains and downplayed its importance. But by the time he picked the letter back up on November 19 from Hackensack, New Jersey, his mood had worsened. He reported the loss of Fort Washington, which had been held against his better judgment. Washington permitted Major General Nathanael Greene to make the final decision to defend the fort. He ended the letter with a powerful line showing his exhaustion: "I am wearied almost to death with the retrog[r]ade Motions of things."[77]

On December 10, Washington again wrote to Lund Washington, updating him on the army's dire situation:

> I wish to Heaven it was in my power to give you a more favourable Acct of our situation . . .
>
> My numbers, till joind by the Philadelphia Militia did not exceed 3000 Men fit for duty—now we may be about 5000 to oppose Howes whole Army . . . I tremble for Philadelphia,

nothing in my opinion but General Lee's speedy arrival . . . can save it. We have brought over, and destroyed, all the Boats we could lay our hands on, upon the Jersey Shore for many Miles above and below this place; but it is next to impossible to guard a Shore for 60 Miles with less than half the Enemys numbers; when by force, or Stratagem they may suddenly attempt a passage in many different places.[78]

Then, more bad news. On December 13, 1776, Washington received word that the British had captured Major General Charles Lee—considered one of the best officers in the Continental Army—while he had been momentarily separated from his troops.[79]

But on December 14, Washington seemed to turn a corner. In a letter to Connecticut Governor Jonathan Trumbull, he described how the enemy's transportation problems had delayed their crossing of the Delaware River. He then mentioned the opportunity for a counterattack:

Whereas by coming on they may, in conjunction with my present Forces and that under Genl Lee enable us to attempt a stroke upon the Forces of the Enemy, who lay a good deal scattered, and to all appearance, in a state of security. A lucky blow in this Quarter would be fatal to them, and would most certainly raise the spirits of the People, which are quite sunk by our late misfortunes.[80] [Note: Though Lee was captured, his forces were not and would join with Washington's main body of troops.]

This is clear written evidence of Washington's decision to attack. While on December 7, British troops were dangerously close—only an hour behind the retreating American forces; then, on December 8, Howe decided to stop his offensive campaign for the season. On December 13, Howe issued an order to put his army into winter quarters. That same day, Washington learned of Lee's capture. The next day, he wrote to Governor Trumbull and characterized the British as "scattered," and suggested a blow "would be fatal."

Despite this renewed determination, Washington still showed flashes of hopelessness. On December 17, he wrote again to Lund Washington:

Our Cause has also receivd a severe blow in the Captivity of General Lee—Unhappy Man! Taken by his own Imprudence!

[Y]our immagination can scarce extend to a situation more distressing than mine—Our only dependance now, is upon the Speedy Inlistment of a New Army; if this fails us, I think the game will be pretty well up[.][81]

Three days later, on December 20, Washington wrote to John Hancock, president of the Continental Congress, in even sharper terms:

[T]en days more will put an end to the existence of our Army . . . [we have made] a mistaken dependance upon Militia, [and they] have been the Origin of all our misfortunes, and the great accumulation of our Debt . . .

[T]he Enemy are daily gathering strength from the disaffected; This strength, like a Snowball by rolling, will increase . . . could any thing but the River Delaware have saved Philadelphia? . . .

[The militia] leave [us] at last at a critical moment. These Sir, are the men, I am to depend upon, Ten days hence . . . In my judgement this is not a time to stand upon expence—our funds are the only Objects of consideration.[82]

He begged for more authority and resources to build a new army. Then, on December 22, Washington received a letter from his aide, Lieutenant Colonel Joseph Reed. Reed had not yet been told about the plan, but he urged Washington to go on the offensive:

> [S]omething must be attempted to revive our expiring Credit give our Cause some Degree of Reputation . . . the scattered divided State of the Enemy affords us a fair Oppy of trying what our Men will do when called to an offensive Attack . . . Something must be attempted before the 60 Days expires.[83]

The very next day, on December 23, Washington responded and informed Reed of the planned attack:

> The bearer is sent . . . to inform you that Christmas day at Night, one hour before day is the time fixed upon for our Attempt on Trenton. For heaven's sake keep this to yourself, as the discovery of it may prove fatal to us . . .
>
> If I had not been fully convinced before of the Enemys designs I have now ample testimony of their Intentions to attack Philadelphia so soon as the Ice will afford the means of conveyance.
>
> P.S. I have orderd our Men to be provided with three days Provisions ready Cook'd; with which, and their Blankets they are to March, for if we are successful which heaven grant & other Circumstances favour we may push on.[84]

This postscript showed Washington was already thinking beyond Trenton. He planned to keep going if possible.

On December 24, he wrote to militia leaders in Connecticut and Massachusetts, telling them to "press" and "march forward with as much expedition as possible to this place or wherever my Head Quarters may be."[85] The phrase "wherever my Head Quarters may be" suggests he expected to be on the move.

That same day, Washington wrote another letter to Hancock, once again pressing the urgent need for supplies and men:

That I should dwell upon the subject of our distresses cannot be more disagreeable to Congress than it is painfull to myself.

[V]ery few of the men have inlisted . . . amounting in the whole at this time from Fourteen to Fifteen hundred effective men. This handfull and such Militia as may chuse to join me will then compose our Army . . .

Genl Howe has a number of Troops cantoned in the Towns bordering on & near the Delaware, his intentions to pass as soon as the ice is sufficiently formed—to invade Pensylvania and possess himself of Philadelphia if possible.[86]

In another dimension, Washington also engaged in somewhat forceful diplomacy. On December 24, he wrote to Native American leaders:

Our Enemy the King of Great Britain endeavoured to Stir up all the Indians from Canada to South Carolina Against Us, But our Bretheren of the Six Nations and their Allies the Shawanese and Delewares would not hearken to the Advice of the Messengers sent among them but kept fast hold of our Ancient Covenant Chain; The Cherokees and the Southern Tribes were foolish enough to listen to them, and to take up the Hatchet Against us,

Upon this our Warriours went into their Country, burnt their Houses, destroyed their Corn, and Oblidged them to sue for peace and give Hostages for their future Good Behaviour.

Now Brothers never lett the Kings Wicked Councellors turn your Hearts Against Me and your Bretheren of this Country . . .[87]

On December 25, Washington issued strict General Orders: Every brigade needed two good guides, and soldiers were to remain silent during the march. No one was allowed to break ranks "on the pain of Death."[88]

Between December 25, 1776, and January 4, 1777, Washington led one of the most celebrated offensives in military history. He crossed the icy Delaware River with 1,400 men and attacked 1,400 Hessian soldiers in Trenton. The other American columns failed to arrive, but Washington's force still struck from two directions. The Hessians were surprised. American losses were minimal (four wounded). They captured 948 enemy troops and killed or wounded another 114. A few days later, Washington attacked again at Princeton. He lost about 44 men as casualties, but killed or captured between 276 and 600 enemy troops (varying estimates from the two sides).[89]

Chapter 5

CONSEQUENCE: WASHINGTON AND HOWE, 1776–1777

The fate of unborn Millions will now depend, under
God, on the Courage and Conduct of this army.
—George Washington (July 2, 1776)

The 1776 campaign showed that the Continental Army could stand against the British. Washington's survival, and his surprise victories at Trenton and Princeton in New Jersey, made major impacts. These victories changed the war.[1] After them, the British could no longer persuade the colonists to come back peacefully. Now, they had to fully conquer the colonies, which was much harder.[2]

Several things resulted from Washington's victories. First, they had a big impact on morale. Before Trenton and Princeton, many colonists had lost hope. But after these victories, even Loyalists noticed the change. Nicholas Cresswell wrote at the time that people had "given up the cause" before those victories, but after them they were "all liberty mad again."[3]

Second, Washington's success gave him more credibility. He used it to ask the states for more troops, who were the key gatekeepers for growing the Continental Army.[4] Eventually, Washington's battlefield success at Trenton and Princeton helped convince Congress to give him that power.[5] Military victories brought political support, which led to more soldiers, which then led to more victories.

His wins also kept soldiers motivated and inspired new ones to join smaller, hit-and-run attacks on the British. Washington had thought about using these "Partizan" or guerilla tactics earlier, having discussed the approach in a war council on July 12, 1776.[6] He had also been influenced by a French book on the tactic called *The Partisan*.[7] After winning at Trenton and Princeton, Washington began using these smaller raids. He even wrote to Major General Philip Schuyler in February 1777 to explain the role these attacks could play. While they were useful, he didn't think they would last forever, saying: "I do not apprehend . . . this Petit Guerre will be continued long. I think Matters will be transacted upon a larger Scale."[8]

Still, Washington's guerilla attacks worked. By the end of winter, Lieutenant General Howe had lost half of his forces in New Jersey.[9] Things got so bad that British soldiers needed fifty guards just to carry a letter between nearby towns. The British lost their ability to gather information and felt surrounded. A few months later, on June 25, 1777, Howe gave up the colony and pulled all his troops out of New Jersey.[10]

Afterward, Washington issued a pardon to colonists who had supported the British. Many accepted, and New Jersey turned against British rule.[11] In short, by surviving and winning battles, Washington broke the idea that the British couldn't be beaten. He also helped the colonists believe in the rebellion again.[12]

These events disrupted British plans for 1777. Lieutenant General Howe's reaction to losing in New Jersey led to British strategic confusion.[13] A month before Trenton and Princeton, on November 30, 1776,

Howe sent a plan to London. It said he would move north to meet up with Major General John Burgoyne, who was coming down from Canada. There was also a plan to fight in the South over the winter. This original plan arrived in London on December 30, 1776.[14]

But after his losses in New Jersey, Howe changed course. He now wanted to capture Philadelphia, where the Continental Congress met.[15] On January 20, 1777, Howe wrote to Lord George Germain that his old plan would not work:

I do not now see a prospect of terminating the war but by a general action . . . the Enemy moves with so much more celerity than we possibly can with our foreign troops who are too much attached to their baggage.[16]

But Howe's change of plans didn't reach London until February 23, 1777. Just five days later, on February 28, Burgoyne's own different plan to march from Canada arrived to Germain.[17] Howe and Burgoyne were not on the same page.

Here, Germain made a serious error. Even though he had seen both plans (from Howe and Burgoyne) and noticed the disconnect, he didn't fix the problem. He had told Howe to work with Burgoyne, but Germain failed to make it happen.[18] Instead of one unified campaign, the British fought two separate, independent campaigns in 1777. Had British forces operated in conjunction with one another, with such resources, and the bulk of the navy at their disposal, Howe and Burgoyne might have defeated the rebels one piece at a time.[19] Washington's victories in New Jersey catalyzed this British confusion.

Once pushed out of New Jersey, Howe wanted a fast win before British resources ran out. He decided to go after Philadelphia by himself and ignored Burgoyne's plan.[20] As a result, Burgoyne was left alone and later lost his army at Saratoga.[21]

As had their losses as Trenton and Princeton, the British loss at Saratoga changed the war. It convinced France to formally join the fight on the American side. France had already been helping the Americans secretly since May 1776. After Saratoga, France ultimately provided significant support through an alliance.[22] Later, Spain joined in 1779, and the Netherlands followed in 1781.[23]

We can see the chain of events. Washington's strategic leadership kept the army alive and forced the British to make bad decisions. Those losses led to the French and others joining the war, which made eventual victory possible. The 1776–1777 campaign was a key moment in Washington's short-term and long-term success.

Washington was not a perfect general, but many have called him a military genius.[24] What made them think so? Some have pointed to his natural understanding of power and how to use it.[25] Others ascribe it to his clear thinking, which avoided distractions and focused on what mattered most.[26] Some believe he had a special talent for making the right choice when facing hard problems.[27]

So what can we learn about strategic leadership from Washington's judgment? And how did traits like empathy and grit help shape his decisions?

One way to measure Washington's strategic leadership is to assess his decisions against those of his main opponent, William Howe. From the start of the campaign, Howe believed the rebels were weak and could be scared into surrender. He didn't try to destroy Washington's army outright. Instead, he wanted to show the Continental Army that it couldn't win. Howe captured a lot of ground, especially in New York, but avoided major battles that could have ended the war quickly. He even offered the Americans several chances to surrender through pardons and peace talks.

Washington had to respond to Howe's strategy. He chose a strategy of exhaustion. He knew his army couldn't defeat the British head on, so he tried to make the war too long and too costly for Britain to keep fighting. He wanted to prove that defeating the colonies would not be worth the effort.

Washington also had to work closely with the Continental Congress. He communicated with them almost daily, balancing military needs with political concerns. When deciding whether to defend or leave New York in the summer of 1776, Washington took Congress's views into account. Some of his generals wanted to burn New York City to hurt the British, but Washington knew this would upset Congress. By handling these disagreements carefully, he gained the trust he needed from Congress and kept his officers loyal. In short, Washington listened.

Our modern strategic leaders—our gray beards—coalesced around this particular trait of Washington's: his openness to truly listen to a wide range of ideas and disagreements, paired with the ability to lock on to a single decision when the time was right. Rear Admiral Studeman asked, "How do you solicit inputs? Because you want all the [organization's] brains engaged, not idle." All of us are smarter than one of us, and it pays to benefit from more brainpower rather than less.

General Neller found it was key for a strategic leader to be "willing to listen, particularly if they have enough self-confidence to let people challenge them." He counseled, "If everybody in the room is agreeing with you all the time, you should really be nervous." He learned this over many, many rounds of going into high-level military briefings. Some, General Neller said, were absolutely terrible, and still "nobody says a word and everybody walks out in the passageway and they go—'I can't believe we're gonna do this.'" That's the cost to shutting out new ideas. Bad ideas can win.

There is, of course, a connected trait: a sort of closedness, a grit. Grit helps a leader decide and stay the course. Grit is the strength to stay steady under pressure, to continue in the face of doubt or pain. Washington showed that grit in December 1776 and January 1777 when he attacked at Trenton and Princeton. His army was depleted, defeat seemed near. Still, he struck twice—at great risk—and revived the revolutionary cause.[28]

Grant and Eisenhower also showed their own flashes of grit at key moments. Grant showed it on May 7, 1864, when, after heavy losses in the Wilderness, he turned his army to fight instead of retreating.[29] It was the beginning of a long, grinding campaign that ultimately led to Union victory. Eisenhower showed grit when he approved the use of airborne drops in the Normandy invasion, despite dire warnings.[30] His decision was risky, but it worked.

In these cases, the strategic leader made a hard decision and stuck with it, even when others strongly disagreed. In the end, there must be one decision-maker, and that role requires an iron gut for tough choices. It means staying firm even when faced with doubt or criticism. Washington had this strength.

Some historians, like Jeremy Black, argue that Washington was "a good political general, rather like Eisenhower. We're not talking about the most astute reader of terrain or topography, and indeed as a battlefield commander he gets it wrong at Long Island."[31]

Criticisms like this divide and conquer. They dismiss the importance of working as a senior military figure within a democratic political system—with all the trade-offs that entails—and simultaneously hammer away at an isolated tactical flaw. But strategic leadership is broader than either of these.

Washington's role wasn't just about battlefield tactics—it was about making better overall decisions than the adversary and keeping the political and military sides of the war working together.

The way we evaluate strategic leadership is by comparing overall results, after the fact, head to head against the adversary. In this case, Washington came out far ahead. He outlasted Howe in the 1776–1777 campaign, survived this toughest stretch of the war, and helped win the whole thing.

Looking at Washington's overall record, especially compared to William Howe's, it's clear that Washington made better judgments. He wasn't perfect in every area. He made mistakes, and he wasn't always the smartest or most skilled in technical matters. But he brought together all the right traits in the right amounts. Especially later in the campaign, when Howe decided to culminate the campaign and Washington decided to attack. That changed the game. The reverse might have been the downfall of the Revolution and America itself.

As historian Edward Lengel has written:

Not so much because he excelled in any particular area—there were better strategists, tacticians, administrators, and politicians among his contemporaries—but because he possessed all of the qualities his country required, and in perfect combination. To survive its difficult birth, America did not just need a courageous soldier, a savvy politician, a hard-working manager, a charismatic leader, a principled believer in democracy, or an intelligent general; it needed all of these things, and in one man. George Washington was that man. No one else could have taken his place.[32]

Washington's success in 1776 also shows that while having more soldiers and weapons matters, it's not everything. What counts more is whether a side has *enough* strength to handle the adversary and still reach its goals. Having more guns is useful and occasionally overwhelming, yet what matters more is if one side has enough guns to deal with the adversary and still obtain some measure of victory.

To win, Washington had to be skilled in every part of warfare—strategy, tactics, leadership, and politics.[33] He had a broad vision, understood the importance of alliances, and worked hard to hold everything together. Absent Washington, there is no victory in this war, and the American idea would have been killed in the crib.

Sometimes wars are won because they are never lost. Battle by battle, Washington may be America's losingest general—but he won the war that mattered the most.

Part III

HOW GRANT WON

Chapter 6

CHALLENGE: GRANT AND LEE, 1864

The odds in favor of Confederate victory were greater than
those in favor of American victory over Britain in 1776.
—Pulitzer Prize–winning historian James McPherson

In February 1861, President-Elect Abraham Lincoln delivered a speech in Trenton, New Jersey. Trenton was the site of George Washington's stunning victory in late December 1776. Reflecting on that earlier struggle, Lincoln said:

There must have been something more than common that those men struggled for . . . something even more than National Independence . . . something that held out a great promise to all the people of the world for all time to come. I am exceedingly anxious that the Union, the Constitution, and the liberties of the people shall be perpetuated in accordance with the original idea for which that struggle was made.[1]

Just two months later, the Civil War began at Fort Sumter, South Carolina—a war that nearly tore America apart.

Both the Union and the Confederacy would invoke the memory of the Revolution to inspire their cause. The Civil War's stakes were at least as high. Without military victory and President Lincoln's reelection in 1864, the United States would have split into two or more separate nations.[2]

Why didn't America break apart in 1864? What decisions brought the war to a close? What did superior strategic leadership contribute to the country's continued existence?

As the winter thawed and spring came in 1864, the Confederacy still controlled a large, contiguous region in the South, much as they had in 1861. Though they had lost key port and river cities like New Orleans and Vicksburg, most major Southern cities remained in Confederate control.

Before Grant was placed in charge of all Union forces, eight generals had held major commands: Winfield Scott, George McClellan, and Henry Halleck served as generals-in-chief. Five others—Irvin McDowell, Ambrose Burnside, John Pope, Joseph Hooker, and George Meade—commanded the main force in the East. Despite their efforts, none brought about true strategic victory. As Lincoln said, "No general yet found can face the arithmetic, but the end of the war will be at hand when he shall be discovered."[3]

So how did Grant succeed when so many others had failed? He later remembered that in the war's Eastern Theater, by 1864, "the opposing forces stood in substantially the same relations towards each other" as they had in 1861.[4] But once Grant was given command, things changed quickly. Assistant Secretary of War Charles Dana wrote: "Grant in eleven months secured the prize with less loss than his predecessors suffered in failing to win it during a struggle of three years."[5]

Some remember Grant differently. Some called him a "butcher" who only won by sacrificing his soldiers.[6] Frank Underwood, main character of political thriller *House of Cards*, put it like this: "Do you know how Grant defeated Lee? He had more men. That's all. He was willing to let them die. It was butchery, not strategy, which won the war."[7]

This view's been repeated by a wide range of people—from First Lady Mary Todd Lincoln to the writers of the "Lost Cause" myth, who claimed as early as 1866 that the South only lost because the North had more resources.[8] In this version, Grant didn't win the war—numbers did.

Of course, numbers did play a role. The Union had more people, more factories, more supplies. But that doesn't explain everything.

Both sides had strengths and weaknesses. The Union included about 22 million people, and roughly 500,000 were enslaved at the start of the war. The Confederacy had around 9 million people, of whom 3 million were enslaved. Two million men fought for the Union—about half of the military-aged male population. In the South, about three-fourths of white males served, supplying the Confederacy with about one million soldiers. This Union manpower advantage carried over into the material domain, where they enjoyed advantages in nearly all other resources required to make war.[9]

The Union also had a working political system, with parties that made decisions through established political processes. The Confederacy didn't have as sturdy a system and struggled at times to make national political and strategic decisions.

Grant's main opponent was Confederate General Robert E. Lee. Lee graduated from West Point in 1829 and had finished second in his class. He was a model cadet who never got a single demerit and was known for spending loads of time in the library. As a cadet, Lee checked out books like:

> *Bland's Algebraical Problems, Bonnycastle's Elements of Geometry,* [Machiavelli's] *Art of War,* Moliere, *Duane's Military Dictionary, Atkinson's Epitome of Navigation, Chastelleux's Travels in North America in 1780, 1781, and 1782, Garden's Anecdotes of the Revolutionary War in America,* Bonaparte's *Sés Mémoires écrits par Montholon et Gourgard,* and many more, including works by Voltaire and Hamilton.[10]

Lee served in the Mexican War and held important posts before the Civil War. When the war began, he was offered a top Union command. But he turned it down because he did not want to fight against his home state. His loyalty to Virginia came first.[11]

Jefferson Davis was the Confederacy's president; Lee, its top military leader. He briefly served as an advisor to Davis but took over command of the Army of Northern Virginia, the main Confederate force, on June 1, 1862. He stayed in that role until the war ended in 1865. Technically, Lee didn't become the Confederacy's "general-in-chief" until late in the war, but it was widely known and accepted that he was in charge of most major military decisions from 1862 on.[12]

Many have called Robert E. Lee a "genius."[13] Historians often praise how he handled the Overland Campaign, saying he was aggressive and skilled even in tough situations.[14] At the height of the war, Lee was deeply admired. A senior surgeon who worked under Lee during the war wrote on July 30, 1864, that Lee was "a genius" and that "no man on this continent or any other now fills so large and important a place to so many people."[15] In early 1865, an Irish visitor to Richmond observed that Lee was "the idol of his soldiers & the Hope of His Country . . . [T]he prestige which surrounds his person & the almost fanatical belief in his judgement & capacity . . . is the one idea of an entire people."[16]

While Lee was seen as a Southern hero, Grant was a more national figure. He was born in Ohio, raised in Missouri and Illinois, and would later say he felt at home anywhere his wife was.[17] Grant went to West Point and graduated in the middle of his class in 1843.[18] After serving in the Mexican War and later in California, Grant left the army in the 1850s. When the Civil War began, he rejoined. He quickly earned success in the Western Theater—he forced a Confederate army to surrender at Fort Donelson in 1862, fought a very tough draw at Shiloh, and captured Vicksburg on July 4, 1863, forcing another Confederate surrender.

In March 1864, after a political debate in Washington, Congress revived the rank of "lieutenant general," and President Lincoln bestowed it upon Grant. This promotion gave Grant supreme command over all Union armies and placed him above all the other major generals who had been promoted earlier.[19] While Lincoln formally appointed him in March, Grant used the time in January and February to think through his plans for the coming 1864 campaign.

In early 1864, Grant considered how to achieve the North's war aims: to keep the Union together and end slavery. At the war's start, Union strategy had followed what became known as the "Anaconda Plan," designed by Brevet Lieutenant General Winfield Scott. It proposed a naval blockade of the South and an accompanying methodical ground campaign. This plan was rejected for being too slow. Then Major General George B. McClellan led the effort to capture Richmond in 1862, planning to build up a massive army to take the Confederate capital. However, this plan dragged on and was never truly executed. Grant would later take Union forces in a new direction in 1864.

The entire 1864 campaign lasted from May into the late fall. Historians usually define the "Overland Campaign" as the continuous fighting through June, but focusing on the longer time frame helps explain how and why the Union ultimately won.[20]

Grant had more troops and supplies than Lee in 1864. But Lee was on the defensive, had the advantage of interior lines for reinforcing troops, and had local knowledge of the terrain that favored his objectives, particularly several rivers that Grant's forces were forced to ford and cross.[21] Lee had led the Army of Northern Virginia for two years and knew his men well. Grant, by contrast, had only just arrived in the Eastern Theater in 1864 after fighting in the West.

The Union had the harder job: to invade, defeat, and occupy an enormous region of about 750,000 square miles, roughly the size of Western Europe (without Spain). The defenders had the advantage. The South also had stronger military traditions, with seven state-level military academies on its side.[22]

Historian Brian Holden Reid has noted that in 1864, just before the campaign began, the Union's main force in the East, the Army of the Potomac, had "95,583 infantry, 15,298 cavalry, 8,000 artillerymen and 274 guns . . . an 'effective' force of 101,895."*[23] Still, that was actually smaller than one year before—when the force under Major General Joseph Hooker had outnumbered Lee by far more than two to one in May 1863 but was defeated at Chancellorsville.[24]

By May 1864, Reid wrote, "Lee could count on 57,811 infantry

---

* "Effective" strength accounts for troops not currently available (i.e., sick, leave, wounded, etc.) and so is not a simple sum of individual components.

and gunners and 8,543 cavalry, plus 200 guns, giving him an 'effective' strength of 61,025 men."[25] So in 1864, Grant's army outnumbered Lee's 1.67 to 1—not as good a gap as Hooker had the year before versus Lee, but still a distinct advantage.

Lee remained a major challenge for Grant.[26] The biggest difference between the two men was age and health. Grant was 42, Lee 57.[27] Years of war had taken a toll on Lee, and he took quite ill during the campaign in late May 1864.[28] Though both led until the war's end, Lee's health was an issue in 1864.

Confederate President Jefferson Davis shaped Southern war policy. His goal was to break away from the Union and create several independent republics where slavery could continue, free from federal interference.[29] The Confederacy needed only to survive to win. That lower bar made a defensive war on home ground seem possible.[30]

Early in the war, the Confederacy executed a "cordon defense"—trying to guard all of its borders. But this strategy failed. It spread their forces too thin and was quickly abandoned. It had been chosen for political purposes, not military logic.

Later, under Lee's leadership, the South adopted an "offensive-defensive" strategy. This meant using tactically offensive thrusts designed to support a wider strategic defensive.[31] But this approach required superior timing—knowing when to strike and when to defend.

For instance, in June 1862, when George McClellan's Union force moved toward Richmond, Lee attacked in the Seven Days Battles and pushed the Union back. Then he continued on the offensive, defeating Union Major General John Pope at the Second Battle of Bull Run in August 1862. He continued his push north until he was stopped at Antietam in September 1862. From 1862 to 1864, Lee often launched these kinds of attacks to try to break Northern support for the war. These raids were part of a larger defensive strategy—aimed at outlasting the Union's will to fight.

COULD THE CONFEDERATES HAVE WON EITHER THIS CAMPAIGN OR THE WAR?

Some say the Confederates never had a chance. They argue the Union's larger population and resources meant the Union was always going to win. Critics who call Grant a "butcher" point to the high Union casualties during the campaign, which did hurt public morale.[32]

One of Grant's early critics, Edward Pollard, wrote in his 1866 book *The Lost Cause* that Grant had "no strategy," and "proposed to decide it by mere competition in the sacrifice of human life." A Richmond newspaper wrote on May 10, 1864, that if Grant ever reached Richmond, he would do so with the "ruins of an army."[33] One of Lee's own officers thought Grant was "beating his head against a wall," and others believed Grant's success came only from superior numbers.[34]

Not everyone agrees. In 2006, a panel of six renowned historians discussed the question "Could the Confederacy Have Won the Civil War?"[35] All six said yes. Pulitzer Prize winner James McPherson wrote: "The odds in favor of Confederate victory were greater than those in favor of American victory over Britain in 1776."[36] Another historian added that the Confederate defeat became certain only after Lincoln's reelection.[37] Why did these experts believe the South might have won?

One way was to wear down the Union's will to fight. If enough Northern voters had grown tired of the war, they might have voted Lincoln out of office in 1864. McPherson considered this the Confederacy's best chance.[38]

Another moment that could have changed the outcome was Major General Jubal Early's raid on Washington, DC, in July 1864. If Early's forces had been more successful, maybe even penetrated the capital city, they might have panicked the Union government or the public.[39]

In early June 1864, after the Union Army of the Potomac's tactical defeat at Cold Harbor, Lincoln's many political rivals, some inside his own cabinet, started pushing to unseat him as the Republican nominee for president.[40] Even Lincoln believed he might lose the coming election. In late August, he wrote a note for his cabinet:

> This morning, and for some days past, it seems exceedingly probable that this Administration will not be re-elected. Then it will be my duty to co-operate with the President elect, as to save the Union between the election and the inauguration; as he will have secured his election on such ground that he can not possibly save it afterwards.[41]

This shows how close things felt at the time, even to Lincoln.

Lincoln knew the Confederacy still had reason to hope.[42] Lee's army believed in him; their morale was strong. Though supplies were tight, Confederate armies never ran out of food or ammunition during the war.[43]

Fighting on home terrain also gave Lee an intelligence advantage.[44] His men knew the land, and defensive positions were easier to hold.[45] In the Civil War, defense was often stronger than offense due to the firepower and limited communication that often made mass attack necessary.

Lieutenant General James Longstreet, one of Lee's top commanders, believed that a strong defense could help the South win in the 1864 election year. He wrote:

If we can break up the enemy's arrangements early, and throw him back, he will not be able to recover his position or his morale until the Presidential election is over, and then we shall have a new President to treat with.[46]

As James McPherson has noted, numbers do not decide wars.[47] And in 1864, even though the Union had the numbers, victory was never a sure thing—until Grant's decisions helped make it so.

Chapter 7

CHOICES AND CLASHES: GRANT AND LEE, 1864

I propose to fight it out on this line if it takes all summer.
—Ulysses S. Grant (May 11, 1864)

HOW SHOULD GRANT ATTACK? HOW SHOULD LEE DEFEND?

Lieutenant General Ulysses S. Grant's first major decision in the 1864 campaign was to attack the Confederacy on all fronts at once. His "general plan" was for all Union armies to act together and "concentrate all the force possible against the Confederate armies in the field."[1] He used the largest Union force—the Army of the Potomac—to keep Lee's Army of Northern Virginia pinned down. Grant judged Lee's army was the Confederacy's main source of strength. While many Union officers feared Lee, Grant respected him but was not overwhelmed by his reputation.[2]

Before officially becoming the Union's supreme commander, Grant workshopped strategy with Major General Henry Halleck, Lincoln's top military adviser. In January 1864, Grant suggested a bold plan: Avoid

Richmond entirely and instead, starting from Suffolk, Virginia, march on Raleigh, North Carolina. Grant thought this would force Lee out of Virginia, allow the Union army to live off the land, and cut off Confederate supplies. Most importantly, it would block Wilmington, North Carolina, a port Grant called "more valuable to the enemy than all the balance of their sea-coast."[3] This plan would widen the fight beyond Virginia and negate some of Lee's key advantages.

Halleck replied that while Richmond wasn't the main goal, he feared public opinion would demand the army be pulled back to protect Northern cities like Washington, Baltimore, and Philadelphia if they were left exposed to Confederate attack. In specific, Halleck relayed that Lincoln did not want Washington unprotected. Halleck wrote that if Grant were to

> uncover Washington and the Potomac River, all the force which Lee can collect will be moved north . . . Lee would tomorrow exchange Richmond, Raleigh, and Wilmington for the possession of either of the aforementioned cities.[4]

Halleck suggested Lee would gladly trade Richmond for an opportunity to threaten Washington. But he misjudged. During the campaign, Lee made it clear he was absolutely committed to defending Richmond. In a letter to his wife, Lee acknowledged, "I begrudge every step [Grant] makes towards Richmond."[5]

Halleck then asked Grant the main question: "The overthrow of Lee's army being the object of operations . . . how can we best attain it?" He then answered his own rhetorical question: "All our available forces in the east should be concentrated against Lee's army."[6]

Halleck favored a focused attack on one area. Grant wanted a different approach—multiple armies attacking from many directions all at once. Grant wanted everything moving, swarming, from all positions, while Halleck preferred a single thrust in a single theater. Multi-directional attrition versus single attack.

So Grant presented Halleck a second plan: simultaneous pressure on all Confederate forces. As Grant explained, "It is my design . . . to work all parts of the army together and somewhat toward a common center."[7]

Around the same time, Grant was more specific in a dispatch to Major General William T. Sherman. Grant said he would direct his subordinate generals as such:

- Nathaniel Banks to move on Mobile, Alabama
- Benjamin Butler to attack Richmond from the Virginia Peninsula
- George G. Meade's Army of the Potomac, with Ambrose Burnside's corps, to attack Lee directly
- Franz Sigel and George Crook to clear the Shenandoah Valley

And to Sherman, Grant wrote: "You I propose to move against Johnston's army . . . inflicting all the damage you can against their war resources."[8]

He then finished with a command similar to his earlier dispatch: "So far as practicable, all the Armies are to move together and towards one common center."[9]

Grant's plan used the Union's advantages in manpower and resources. He wanted to pressure all Confederate armies at once, to stretch them thin and prevent them from helping one another. His strategy was not only military—it was political, too. Victories needed to boost Union morale, but they couldn't be so costly that the public turned against the war. Grant had to balance battlefield wins with political support at home.[10]

The campaign began on May 5, 1864, with the Battle of the Wilderness. Lee already had a plan to be aggressive. That February 3, he had written about taking "the initiative," to "derange [Union] plans & embarrass them."[11] In March, he wrote he would "concentrate wherever they are going to attack us."[12] Lee chose to fight in the Wilderness, where the dense forest would partially offset the Union size advantage. When the battle ended, Lee had lost around 11,125 men as casualties (total killed, wounded, and missing). Grant lost even more—17,666.[13]

Still, Grant didn't stop. He kept moving forward. In addition to attacking everywhere, his second key decision was sheer relentlessness. Grant wouldn't retreat after setbacks. William T. Sherman described this moment as the most important in Grant's life:

> On the night of May 7th both parties paused, appalled by the fearful slaughter; but General Grant commanded "Forward by the left flank." That was, in my judgment, the supreme moment of his life: undismayed, with a full comprehension of the importance of the work in which he was engaged, feeling as keen a sympathy for his dead and wounded as anyone, and without stopping to count his numbers, he gave his orders calmly, specifically, and absolutely—"Forward to Spotsylvania."[14]

That same day, Grant told a reporter: "If you see the President, tell him, from me, that, whatever happens, there will be no turning back."[15]

Grant was in the same situation Union Major General Joseph Hooker had faced one year earlier—after a costly battle on almost exactly the same terrain. Hooker was defeated in battle but after the fight still had more men and still pulled back. Grant pushed forward. Earlier Union generals—McClellan, Burnside, Hooker, Meade—had seen similar setbacks as defeats. Grant saw them as part of the process.[16] Lincoln praised this: "If any other general had been at the head of that army it would now have been on this side of the Rapidan [River]. It is the dogged pertinacity of Grant that wins."[17]

Still, the campaign stalled again in early June at the Battle of Cold Harbor. Grant's army suffered around 6,000 losses, Lee's between 1,000 and 1,500.[18] Grant admitted tactical defeat and wrote, "Without a greater sacrifice of human life than I am willing to make all cannot be accomplished."[19]

He knew he had to try something else. Grant wrote to his father that Lee's forces were "always on the defensive and strongly intrenched."[20] So Grant turned back to his original plan, an indirect strike at the Confederate source of strength.[21] He wrote to Halleck:

> My idea from the start has been to beat Lee's Army, if possible, North of Richmond . . . [then] to transfer the Army to the South side and besiege Lee in Richmond, or follow him South if he should retreat.[22]

So Grant moved to the south side of the James River. He explained his next goal: to "cut off all sources of supply to the enemy except what is furnished by [their water-borne logistical lines]."[23] Since Lee's army was well protected around Richmond and Petersburg, Grant focused on destroying logistics—especially railroads—that kept the Confederate armies supplied.

At the same time, Grant gave key support roles to major generals William T. Sherman and Philip Sheridan. He sent Sheridan on a raid with over 10,000 cavalry against Confederate cavalry and Richmond itself—despite protests from Major General George Meade, who wanted to keep cavalry assets for his own Army of the Potomac.[24] But Grant explained Sheridan's mission had three goals:

"First," it would cut off enemy supplies and communication and possibly secure useful supplies for the Union.

"Second," it would draw away Confederate cavalry and protect Union flanks.

"Third," Sheridan's absence would reduce the army's need for supplies from Fredericksburg, which had become the Union's base.[25]

Sheridan's raid was a success. It killed famed Confederate cavalry leader Major General J. E. B. Stuart. Lee later told President Jefferson Davis that such a loss was a serious threat: "I cannot but entertain serious apprehensions about the safety of our southern communications."[26]

Sheridan's success provided Grant greater latitude after a meeting with President Lincoln on July 31, 1864. Grant ordered Sheridan "to put himself south of the enemy and follow [the Confederates] to the death. Wherever the enemy goes let ou[r] troops go also."[27] Sheridan took command of a new army of 45,000 soldiers from several corps.[28] Though Lincoln's chief military adviser, Henry Halleck, doubted the plan, Lincoln thought it "exactly right" and supported it, writing to Grant, "It will neither be done nor attempted unless you . . . force it."[29]

Sheridan's troops attacked into the Shenandoah Valley, a major supply source for the Confederacy.[30] As promised, he left "little in it for man or beast."[31] His raid was a critical support to Grant's overall strategy.

Meanwhile, Sherman tore through Georgia. His campaign left a path of destruction up to 60 miles wide. Just days after the Democratic Party nominated former Union commander George McClellan to run against Lincoln in the 1864 election, Sherman captured Atlanta on September 2, 1864.[32]

To Union citizens, cities like Atlanta were signs of victory. Sherman's success in Georgia was proof that Grant's strategy was working and helped boost support for Lincoln's reelection. Still, Grant wasn't satisfied. A week later, he wrote to Sherman: "We want to keep the enemy continually pressed to the end of the war . . . the end cannot be distant."[33]

Grant gave clear instructions to his generals. In October 1864, he told Sherman: "Destroy . . . all of military value in Atlanta."[34] That same month, he told Sheridan to: "threate[n] the Va. Central rail-road & Canal . . . If you make the enemy hold a force equal to your own for the protection of those thoroughfares it will accomplish nearly as much as their destruction."[35]

These messages show Grant wasn't focused on capturing land—he aimed to end the Confederacy's ability to fight. Grant's strategy caused serious problems for Lee. Lee had to pull reinforcements to his formation from other Southern armies—over 24,000 men in total.[36] That weakened areas where Sherman marched. The Confederacy was running out of men. Grant's pressure worked.

Lee also lost many of his most trusted commanders.[37] Major General J. E. B. Stuart was killed. Lieutenant General James Longstreet was badly wounded. Lieutenant General A. P. Hill became ill, and Lieutenant General Richard Ewell was removed from command. In just the first eight days of fighting in May 1864, Lee's force lost over one-third of its top commanders.[38] The Union lost far fewer. These losses hit Lee hard and showed the power of Grant's approach.

From the start of the campaign at the Battle of the Wilderness, Grant pinned Lee's army in place.[39] He then threatened the Confederacy's remaining field armies—Lee's last chance to force a favorable peace.[40] Grant's offensives pushed Lee into a corner in Petersburg, where he had to protect Richmond, his army, and the Confederacy's last working railroad.[41] After this, Lee had no ability to go on the offensive. Grant's strategy of attrition—wearing down the enemy—was working. Of course, Grant's campaign came at a high cost. From May through early June 1864, the Union lost about 55,000 soldiers.[42] Lee lost about 33,000. Grant's losses were roughly 45% of his initial force, and Lee lost over half of his men.[43] While Grant lost many soldiers, so did Lee. But Lee couldn't replace them.

Historian Edward Bonekemper explained how hard Grant's attacks hit Lee's army. Major General Ewell's Second Corps started the campaign with 17,000 men and had just 6,000 left after the campaign's first two battles.[44] Ewell was relieved shortly after.

These enormous losses shocked the Northern public, who were preparing to vote in the 1864 presidential election. For the first time, Americans saw sustained high casualty numbers over several weeks.[45] Grant knew how bad it looked. He later wrote:

> The losses inflicted, and endured, were destined to be severe; but the armies now confronting each other had already been in deadly conflict for a period of three years, with immense losses . . . and neither had made any real progress toward accomplishing the final end . . . but the carnage was to be limited to a single year, and to accomplish all that had been anticipated or desired at the beginning in that time.[46]

Grant believed the cost was bearable to achieve such a crucial outcome. While the casualties were politically dangerous, the net result mattered more. Grant broke Lee's strategy and took away his chance to win.

This wasn't just a bloody campaign—it was a strategic victory.[47] Grant kept the initiative, and that, against an exceptional commander like Lee, was no small feat.[48]

Lieutenant General Robert E. Lee is often seen as the most important figure in the Confederate war effort. He was admired by many Southerners on par with George Washington, a figure who had attained a mythical status.[49] At the end of the war, one of his generals, Henry A. Wise, told Lee, "There has been no country, general, for a year or more. You are the country to these men. They have fought for you."[50] To many, Lee was the heart of the Confederate cause.

But this fame came with a price. The Army of Northern Virginia, under Lee's command, became the main target for the Union's Army of the Potomac. While Lee thought Richmond was the Union's primary goal, Union forces focused on defeating Lee's army. Most Confederate military resources were spent supporting Lee's army, which remained committed to protecting Richmond.

Lee believed he could weaken the Union's will to fight. In a letter to his wife in 1863 before the Battle of Chancellorsville, he wrote:

> If we can baffle them in their various designs this year & our people are true to our cause & not so devoted to themselves & their own aggrandizement, I think our success will be certain . . . If successful this year, next fall there will be a great change in public opinion at the North. The Republicans will be destroyed & I think the friends of peace will become so strong as that the next administration will go in on that basis. We have only therefore to resist manfully.[51]

This explains Lee's offensive-defensive strategy. Launch limited attacks aimed at discouraging Union morale, while more broadly defending the Confederacy until the Union quit the war. He followed this principle during raids north at Antietam in 1862 and Gettysburg in 1863. And he still believed in it going into the 1864 campaign. On February 3, 1864, Lee wrote to President Jefferson Davis: "If we could take the initiative & fall upon them unexpectedly we might derange their plans & embarrass them the whole summer."[52]

Lee asked for more troops because he believed he could ruin Union plans, no matter how large the enemy force. He wanted to fight aggressively, even when the odds were far from in his favor.[53] Lee also made assumptions about Union strength. In a letter to Davis on April 5, 1864, just before the Battle of the Wilderness, Lee wrote:

> All the information I receive tends to show that the great effort of the enemy in this campaign will be made in Virginia . . . They cannot collect the large force they mention for their operations against Richmond without reducing their other armies.[54]

Lee thought that if Grant sent a large army to Virginia, Union forces elsewhere would weaken. This proved false. Grant's forces in Virginia remained substantial without hurting other Union armies (such as those led by Sherman and Sheridan).

Lee's desire to attack continued throughout the campaign. On May 11, he wrote to Brigadier General Henry Heth, saying he believed Grant might withdraw and that "we must attack those people if they retreat."[55] Even when sick and bedridden during the Battle of the North Anna River, Lee insisted, "We must strike them a blow."[56]

On May 23, Lee wrote to Davis, saying: "It seems to me our best policy [is] to unite upon [Grant's army] and endeavor to crush it."[57] At that point, the Confederate Army of Northern Virginia had about 51,000 soldiers, while the Union Army of the Potomac had 67,000.[58] Though Grant began the campaign with a 1.67-to-1 advantage, the gap had narrowed. The numbers were close enough to cause Lee to believe an attack might succeed.

Even in June, Lee continued thinking offensively. On June 4, he wrote to Lieutenant General Richard Anderson (who had assumed command from the wounded Lieutenant General James Longstreet): "I apprehend . . . [Grant] is preparing to leave us tonight . . . In that event . . . [we should] move down and attack him with our whole force."[59]

While Lee remained focused on attack, he also kept one eye on Richmond.[60] Back in December 1863, President Davis had offered Lee a command in the West, but Lee declined.[61] He wanted to stay near Virginia and defend the Confederate capital.

Lee wasn't wrong to focus on the East. Lincoln saw it as the war's main theater. In August 1862, after a Union victory in the West, Lincoln wrote: "It seems unreasonable that a series of successes . . . should help us so little, while a single half-defeat should hurt us so much."[62] The world paid much more attention to what happened in Virginia than what happened elsewhere.

Before the campaign commenced, Lee again warned Davis about Grant's movements on April 15, 1864:

> I think it certain that the enemy is organizing a large army . . . intended to move directly on Richmond . . . If Richmond could be held secure against the attack from the east, I would propose that I draw Longstreet to me & move right against the enemy on the Rappahannock. Should God give us a crowning victory there,

all their plans would be dissipated . . . I however see no better plan for the defense of Richmond than that I have proposed.[63]

On May 4, he wrote again to Davis: "[I]t is apparent that the long threatened effort to take Richmond has begun, and that the enemy has collected all his available force to accomplish it."[64]

By the end of May, Lee was worried about his ability to hold the city.[65] On May 30, 1864, he wrote to Davis: "If this army is unable to resist Grant, the troops [assigned to] the city will be unable to defend [Richmond alone]."[66]

Some argue that Lee was too narrowly focused and tied too closely to Virginia. Others have defended Lee, saying he was not an outdated thinker and that he put national goals ahead of local ones. Either way, Lee's dispatches and orders show he was determined to fight offensively to protect Richmond. He also believed that if Grant was strong in Virginia, other parts of the Union army must be vulnerable to other Confederate forces—an assumption that turned out to be wrong.[67]

In the end, Lee's decisions gave the Union exactly what it needed—a confident, offensively focused opponent who kept fighting with fewer and fewer resources. And as Grant pressed, Lee's options narrowed. His army, his supplies, and his hopes all wore down together.[68]

SHOULD LEE RAID WASHINGTON? IF SO, HOW SHOULD GRANT DEFEND WASHINGTON?

While Lieutenant General Grant stayed on the strategic offensive in 1864, General Robert E. Lee launched a tactical offensive by ordering a raid on Washington, DC. In mid-June, Lee sent Lieutenant General

Jubal Early and his corps through the Shenandoah Valley toward the Union capital.[69]

The raid caused panic in Washington and cast doubt on President Lincoln's leadership. Its timing was critical—it happened during the buildup to the 1864 election and at a moment when it seemed possible to throw the Northern election away from Lincoln.[70] Northern newspapers warned of danger with headlines like "THE CAPITAL SERIOUSLY THREATENED" and reported that "a very large force of rebels" was closing in on the city.[71]

Lee gave Early the order to raid Washington on June 12, 1864.[72] At the time, Confederate defenses around Richmond were stretched thin over a 35-mile front.[73] A raid on Washington might relieve pressure, force Grant to pull troops back, and damage Northern morale. Lee had hinted at this idea earlier. In a dispatch to Lieutenant General A. P. Hill in May, Lee wrote: "The time has arrived . . . when something more is necessary than adhering to lines and defensive positions."[74]

As Grant closed in, Lee feared a long siege and began exploring other options. In early June, Major General Braxton Bragg suggested to Confederate President Jefferson Davis that they try to clear Union forces from the Shenandoah Valley and open the road to Washington.[75] On June 11, the day before Early departed, Lee shared his concerns with Davis: "It would [take] one corps of this army . . . If it is deemed prudent to hazard the defense of Richmond . . . I will do so. I think this is what the enemy would desire."[76]

Though hesitant, Lee agreed to the raid. He thought the only alternative was to attack Grant's strong defenses around Richmond—an action that might risk everything. Lee concluded: "To attack him here I must assault a very strong line of intrenchments and run great risk to the safety of the army."[77]

Jubal Early left on June 15, and Lee reported: "Genl Early was in motion this morning at 3 o'clock . … His troops would make us more secure here, but success in the Valley would relieve our difficulties."[78] Lee hoped the raid would draw Grant's attention, give the Confederates breathing room, and perhaps even turn the political tide in the North.

Early said his mission was "to strike" and "if possible, destroy" Union forces in the Valley and then "threaten Washington City." His corps had about 8,000 soldiers. On the way to Washington, another unit joined him, which brought his force to around 12,000 men.[79]

As Early moved through Maryland, he took supplies and demanded $200,000 from the citizens of Frederick. He then ran into a small Union force led by Major General Lew Wallace.[80] Wallace had just 6,300 men, many raw recruits. On July 9, 1864, Wallace tried to stop Early at the Battle of Monocacy. Wallace lost and withdrew to Baltimore, suffering around 1,300 casualties to Early's 800. But Wallace's effort delayed Early long enough for Union reinforcements to arrive in Washington.

On July 10, Early approached Fort Stevens, one of the capital's outer defenses.[81] At that time, Washington may have been the most heavily defended capital in the world. Among its defenses were "68 enclosed forts boast[ing] 807 mounted cannon and 93 mortars in 1,120 emplacements . . . plus 20 miles of rifle trenches and three blockhouses."[82]

On July 11, Lee informed Early that Union reinforcements were arriving and left it up to him to decide whether to attack based on "the circumstances."[83] Grant had dispatched a corps with an extra division to protect the city, and Wallace's stand bought time for those troops to arrive.[84]

The mood in Washington was tense. It felt like Union sentiment might turn against the war.[85] President Lincoln even visited Fort Stevens to observe the situation firsthand. Historian James McPherson wrote,

"The six-foot-four-inch president wearing his top hat made a large target as he peered over the parapet at enemy sharpshooters . . . A Union officer was shot while standing close to the president."[86]

The Battle of Fort Stevens ended with around 1,000 total casualties, roughly equal on both sides.[87] Early had shaken Union morale just five weeks before Lincoln would write his famous August 23, 1864, cabinet memo predicting he might lose reelection.

Confederate newspapers praised the raid. Some Confederates believed it might increase Union demands for peace. But others thought it could have the opposite effect—to make the Union more determined, more resolute.[88]

When Lieutenant General Early launched his raid on Washington, Lieutenant General Ulysses S. Grant didn't panic. Instead, he saw the raid as a chance to attack Confederate troops while they were outside strong defensive lines. On July 5, 1864, Grant wrote to Halleck, fully aware of Early's movements: "We want now to crush out & destroy any force the enemy dares send north. Force enough can be spared from here to do it."[89]

President Lincoln, however, was more alarmed. Newspapers called Early's movement "the Rebel Invasion," and public concern grew.[90] Lincoln feared Washington was at risk and asked Grant to leave a small force to hold the siege lines at Richmond and Petersburg, while bringing most of the Union army back to defend the capital.[91]

Grant disagreed. He saw Early's raid as more distraction than threat. On July 10, Grant wrote to Lincoln explaining why he would not return in person: "I think on reflection it would have a bad effect for me to leave here . . . I have great faith that the enemy will never be able to get back with much of his force."[92]

Instead of rushing back, Grant decided to send one corps plus an additional division to help defend Washington. He believed the force Lee sent under Early wasn't strong enough to seriously threaten the capital or change the war's outcome. Grant had already tied down Lee's main force at Richmond and Petersburg, and other Union armies were pushing hard against Confederate forces across the South. From Grant's perspective, a smaller, well-timed parry was enough.[93]

Grant's judgment proved correct. Early's raid caused anxiety in the North, but it did not break Washington's defenses. By the middle of July, Early was gone, and the Union remained on offense. Two key Confederate forces—Lee's in Richmond and Johnston's (later Hood's) in Atlanta—were stuck in place.[94] Grant wrote confidently on July 5, 1864: "If the rebellion is not perfectly and thoroughly crushed, it will be the fault and through the weakness of the people [of the] North. Be of good cheer and rest assured that all will come out right."[95]

Not everyone shared Grant's confidence. By August, Major General Halleck wanted to scale back Union operations due to the high casualties and slow pace of progress.[96] Grant strongly disagreed. He wrote to Congressman Elihu Washburne on August 16, explaining why the Union had to stay the course:

> The rebels have now in their ranks their last man . . . A man lost by them cannot be replaced. They have robbed the cradle and the grave equally to get their present force . . . They are now losing from desertions and other causes at least one regiment per day. With this drain upon them the end is visible if we will but be true to ourselves. Their only hope now is in a divided North.[97]

Grant understood that the Confederate strategy depended on outlasting Union will, not just winning battles. He believed that holding firm through the summer and into the election would deliver victory.

HOW SHOULD LEE REQUEST PRISONER EXCHANGE? HOW SHOULD GRANT SUPPORT THE SOLDIER VOTE?

As the campaign continued, General Robert E. Lee found himself short on troops and sought ways to strengthen the Confederate Army of Northern Virginia. On October 1, 1864, he wrote to Lieutenant General Ulysses S. Grant and asked for a prisoner exchange.[*][98]

Grant replied the next day, October 2, with a rebuttal:

I could not of a right accept your proposition further than to exchange those prisoners captured within the last three days . . . Among those lost by the Armies operating against Richmond were a number of Colored troops. Before further negociations are had upon the subject I would ask if you propose delivering these men the same as White soldiers.[99]

Grant's response revealed the real issue with Lee's offer. Lee wasn't merely concerned with getting soldiers back. He saw the exchange as a way to influence Northern politics—especially with the presidential election just a month away. Lee knew that some border state Unionists still supported slavery. By refusing to exchange Black soldiers equally, Lee

---

[*]   Note: In the dispatches that follow, there are a great many written inaccuracies by the hand of each strategic leader; so many that to include notation for each would significantly increase the size of each entry. As such, they have been left as originally written.

hoped to stir political tension. Lee's message to the Union: *White soldiers are suffering in captivity for Black soldiers.*

Grant rejected Lee's attempt. He knew Lee's goal was to regain manpower and sow division. Grant chose to deny Lee both. He wouldn't allow Confederate forces to regain soldiers, even if it meant Union prisoners remained in captivity. Grant also understood that standing firm on equality for Black soldiers would further isolate the Confederates in the eyes of the world.

On October 3, Lee replied:

In my proposition of ~~yesterday~~ of the 1st Inst: to exchange the prisoners of War belonging to the armies operating in Viga I intended to include all captured soldiers of the U.S. of whatever nation Colour under my Control – Deserters from our Service, & negroes belonging to our Citizens ~~are were~~ are not Considered Subjects of exchange & ~~are~~ were not included in my proposition. If there are any Such among those stated by you to have been Captured around Richmond, & they ~~will~~ can not be ~~exchanged~~ returned.[100]

Here, Lee made clear that formerly escaped enslaved people who had joined the Union army would not be returned. His language was deliberately vague, allowing Confederate officers to decide who would be considered eligible for exchange. Grant responded immediately: "The Government is bound to secure all persons received into her Armies the rights due to soldiers. This being denied by you . . . induces me to decline making the exchanges you ask."[101] He said the matter would be referred to higher authorities, but that the Union would stand by its principles.

Grant's decision fit within his larger strategy. He had written to Secretary of War Edwin Stanton on September 13, 1864:

> Prompt action in filling our Armies will have more effect upon the enemy than a victory over them. They profess to believe, and make their men believe, there is such a party North in favor of recognizing southern independence that the draft can not be enforced. ~~Undeceive them and you gain a great triumph~~ Let them be undeceived. Deserters come into our lines daily who tell us that the men are nearly universally tired of the War and that desertions would be much more frequent but they believe peace will be negotiated after the fall elections. The enforcement of the draft and prompt filling ~~of~~ up of our Armies will save the shedding of bloods to an immence degree.[102]

Grant assessed the political risks and championed the no-exchange policy.[103] But he believed the long-term benefit was clear: "It is hard on our men held in Southern prisons not to exchange them, but it is humanity to those left in our ranks to fight in our battles."[104]

And in a message to Secretary of State William H. Seward, Grant made his view even more direct: "We have got to fight until the Military power of the South is exhausted and if we release or exchange prisoners captured it simply becomes a War of extermination."[105]

Grant chose a harder path, one that aligned with both military strategy and moral principle. His decision not to exchange prisoners weakened the Confederate army and kept the Union's goal in focus: total victory.

Lieutenant General Ulysses S. Grant understood the Civil War was not just a military contest—it was a political one as well. While he worked to stop General Robert E. Lee's push for a prisoner exchange, he also used military policy to support the reelection of President Abraham Lincoln in 1864.

Grant believed strongly that politics matters at war. He once said that politics were an "ever-present consideration," and although he had strong opinions, he said he "took no open part in politics" and "never allowed" himself to be influenced by them. In his view, "political bias" was "fatal to a soldier," and a soldier had "no right" to interfere in the political process.[106]

Even though Grant did not vote in the 1864 election, he supported Lincoln's reelection in every legal and ethical way.[107] He believed that absent Lincoln's leadership—if McClellan were to win the presidency—the Union would not survive.

Lincoln faced real political danger. In the 1862 midterm elections, Lincoln's Republican Party had lost 23 House seats, dropping from 59% control to just 46%, which meant they lost the House majority. Over the next two years, newspapers reported Lee's continued military success, while some Republicans broke away to form the "Radical Republicans," claiming Lincoln wasn't tough enough on the South or committed enough to abolishing slavery.[108]

Grant knew how tenuous Lincoln's political position had become. The president's loss would change the war's outcome.

Without public polls, Grant couldn't know how the election would go. He never campaigned, but he allowed Lincoln to use his official military updates to inform the public. Grant wrote to Lincoln supporter Elihu Washburne: "I have no objection to the President using any thing I have ever written to him as he sees fit—I think however for him to attempt to answer all the charges the opposition will bring against him will be like setting a maiden to work to prove her chastity."[109]

In late September 1864, Grant wrote to Secretary of War Edwin Stanton to express his full support for the soldier vote in the field. Grant acknowledged that it was "a novel thing" and that some believed it was "dangerous to constitutional liberty and subversive of Military discipline."[110]

But Grant argued the situation was unique:

[The] circumstances are novel and exceptional. A very large proportion of the legal voters of the United States, are now either under arms in the field, or in hospitals, or otherwise engaged in the Military service of the United States . . . they are American Citizens, having still their homes and social and political ties, binding them to the States and Districts, from which they come, and to which they expect to return. They have left their homes temporarily, to sustain the cause of their country, in the hour of its trial. In performing this sacred duty, they should not be deprived of a most precious privilege. They have as much right to demand that their votes shall be counted, in the choice of their rulers, as those citizens, who remain at home; Nay more, for they have sacrificed more for their country.[111]

Grant stressed the importance of fairness and discipline. He wrote: "The Officers and Soldiers . . . have every means of understanding the questions before the country. The newspapers are freely circulated." And to ensure neutrality, Grant ordered there would be "no political meetings, no harangues from soldiers or citizens and no canvassing of camps or regiments for votes."[112]

In mid-October, Grant told Halleck to issue a general order for all soldiers on recruiting duty to return to their units so they could vote in person in their home states.[113]

Grant also viewed the election as a potential battlefield opportunity. On November 5, 1864, he warned Major General George G. Meade (commander of the main Union Army of the Potomac) that the Confederates might use the election as a chance to launch a surprise attack.[114] He worried they might try to stop the vote or catch Union forces off guard. Two days later, he wrote to Brevet Major General Alfred Terry of the Army of the James: "There is sufficient probability of you being attacked to justify requiring the greatest vigilance . . . If the enemy should attack and be repulsed he should be followed up at once and no officer should hold back for orders to do so."[115]

Secretary of War Stanton also asked Grant to allow Delaware soldiers stationed near Petersburg to go home to vote. These regiments were small, but their votes might decide the state.[116] Grant replied: "If possible I will give the furloughs you ask. Will telegraph you again in the course of the day tomorrow."[117] A few days later, Grant sent those three Delaware regiments home to vote.[118]

On election day, as results began to come in, Grant sent word to Stanton with internal poll numbers from the Army of the Potomac.[119] Early results favored Lincoln, and he did, of course, win the election of 1864.

Lincoln reflected not long after in his annual message to Congress, "The election has exhibited another fact not less valuable to be known—the fact that we do not approach exhaustion in the most important branch of national resources, that of living men."[120]

Lincoln's reelection marked a turning point. General Lee had hoped to divide the Union, but that strategy had failed.

Although Lincoln beat Democratic candidate and Major General George B. McClellan with 55% of the popular vote and 212 Electoral College votes to McClellan's 21, the victory was no blowout. Lincoln won 78% of the soldier vote in an estimate of 12 of the states, but only 53% of the civilian vote in those same 12.[121] The soldier vote mattered.

Historian Edward Bonekemper has noted just how close the race was: "A shift of less than one percent of the popular vote (29,935 out of 4,031,195) could have given McClellan an additional 97 electoral votes—enough to provide him with the 118 electoral votes he needed to win."[122]

On election day, Charles Francis Adams Jr., serving in the Union cavalry, wrote to his brother: "This election has relieved us of the fire in the rear and now we can devote an undivided attention to the remnants of the Confederacy."[123]

Just days later, on November 18, 1864, Lee admitted: "Desertion is increasing in the army despite all my efforts to stop it."[124] With the political war won, the military side of the war was all but over.

Grant sent congratulations to Lincoln through Stanton: "Congratulate the President for me for the double victory. The election having passed off quietly, no bloodshed or riot throughout the land, is a victory worth more to the country than a battle won. Rebeldom and Europe both will feel it—will so construe it."[125]

It was so because Grant listened, learned, and adjusted his approach. Because he chose constant, multifront pressure. Because he was persistent after setbacks. And because Grant wore Lee's Confederates down—the war was won.

Chapter 8

CONSEQUENCE: GRANT AND LEE, 1864

*The issue is distinct, simple, and inflexible. It is an issue
which can only be tried by war and decided by victory.*
—Abraham Lincoln (December 6, 1864)

In May 1864, both the Union and the Confederacy still had a chance to win the war. The South still held most of its territory, and the Union had not yet taken control of large areas in the South. Seven months later—by mid-November—the situation had changed. Why?

Because Grant pinned Lee's army down.[1] Lee was no longer able to go on the attack or use his preferred offensive-defensive strategy. Instead, Lee had to stay in place and defend, while Grant applied continuous pressure and forced Lee into difficult choices that hurt the South's chances.

Then Union forces took Atlanta and the Shenandoah Valley.

These victories helped secure President Abraham Lincoln's reelection and showed that the Confederacy no longer had any hope of winning. Grant's 1864 campaign changed the game and made this happen. From then on, only a few minor skirmishes remained—like the Battle of Five Forks—before Lee surrendered at Appomattox in April 1865.

Grant's forces caused heavy losses to Lee's army—losses they couldn't replace. Lee knew this. On August 23, 1864—the same day Lincoln wrote that he fully expected to lose the election—Lee wrote to the Confederate Secretary of War, James Seddon: "Without some increase in our strength, I cannot see how we are to escape the natural military consequences of the enemy's numerical superiority."[2]

Later, on September 2, 1864, Lee warned Confederate President Jefferson Davis:

As matters now stand, we have no troops disposable to meet movements of the enemy or strike where opportunity presents, without taking them from the trenches or exposing some important point.[3]

Grant's overall strategy—attacking on several fronts at once—allowed Union generals Sherman and Sheridan freedom of action. Grant helped set up Sherman's capture of Atlanta on September 2, and Sheridan's destruction of the Shenandoah Valley, which had been a major source of Confederate supplies and a path for invading the North.[4] Without Grant keeping Lee's Army of Northern Virginia tied down, these victories would not have happened.[5]

Grant also understood the political pressures of 1864. He had to defend Washington, apply enough pressure on Lee to weaken the Confederacy, and keep Northern morale high enough to ensure Lincoln's reelection.[6] He managed all three.

His closest wartime partner, William T. Sherman, may have understood Grant's command best.

Not quite two years after Grant's death, Sherman penned an essay in *The North American Review* to rebut an article written by British Field Marshal Garnet Wolseley (then serving as commander-in-chief of British forces, and who had observed some of the American Civil War from the Confederate side) in March 1887. Wolseley had read Robert E. Lee's memoirs, and found that:

General Lee towered far above all men on either side in that struggle. I believe he will be regarded, not only as the most prominent figure of the Confederacy, but as the great American of the nineteenth century, whose statue is well worthy to stand on an equal pedestal with that of Washington, and whose memory is equally worthy to be enshrined in the hearts of all his countrymen.[7]

Sherman disagreed completely with Wolseley's characterization, and in a rebuttal wrote that Lee's

sphere of action was, however, local. He never rose to the grand problem which involved a continent and future generations. His Virginia was to him the world. Though familiar with the geography of the interior of this great continent, he stood like a stone wall to defend Virginia . . . He stood at the front porch battling with the flames whilst the kitchen and house were burning, sure in the end to consume the whole.

Sherman continued: "Grant's 'strategy' embraced a continent, Lee's a small State . . . Grant had to conquer natural obstacles . . . his 'tactics' were to fight wherever and whenever he could . . . When Lee laid down his arms . . . Grant . . . gave him . . . terms so liberal as to disarm all criticism."

Sherman ended: "Between these two men as generals . . . I will not institute a comparison, for the mere statement of the case establishes a contrast."[8]

Sherman pointed out an essential fact from the duel between these two giants. One won a lasting victory, and the other did not.

Grant and the Union had more people and resources, and their government was more stable. But they also had the harder job: They had to attack, defeat the Confederate armies, and take back huge areas of land. The Confederates fought hard, and they had enough soldiers and support to keep going. Lee's goal wasn't to conquer the North—it was just to survive long enough for the North to give up. He had chances to do that.

Grant's 1864 campaign brought the war to a successful conclusion, a clear case in superior strategic leadership. Equally important in our modern world is what we might learn.

One way Grant's thinking echoes in our modern strategic leaders is the acknowledgment that they must always be mindful that there are no fixed rules in warfare or competition.

Some generals, Grant felt, "failed because they worked out everything by rule. They knew what Frederick did at one place, and Napoleon at another. They were always thinking about what Napoleon would do." But such consideration meant they were thinking less about present realities and their immediate opponent. Grant said he did not "underrate the value of military knowledge," but that "if men make war in slavish observance to rules, they will fail." To do so meant that, too often, "practical facts were neglected," which, strictly in this case, Grant considered

remembrances of old campaigns a disadvantage. Even Napoleon showed that, for my impression is that his first success came because he made war in his own way, and not in imitation of others. War is progressive, because all the instruments and elements of war are progressive.[9]

Put another way, you can never learn how to "win wars." You can only hope to win the war you're in.

When I asked General Austin Miller about his approach to strategy, he noted the importance of "really try[ing] to get down to the essence of 'What are we doing? And why are we doing it?'" Then, "if we agree on those first questions—do our actions actually make sense? Or are there other actions to be taken?" He had a real practical, problem solver's approach to strategy, and was fairly dismissive of those who see themselves as "real strategic" but don't have their finger on the pulse of a particular problem. General Miller described strategy almost as an unbroken short line from the top-end, highest objectives, down to the tactical end where the job gets done. He felt strongly that a strategic leader has "to do both"—to see the wide and deep picture including both the strategic horizon and the tactical fight.

Curiosity is a strategic advantage here. A willingness to see things anew, rather than lazily falling back on old strategies or ideas that don't fit the situation. General Miller asked a provocative but important question. Now that drones have become a routine feature in modern war, he asked, "How many senior leaders have drones in their home? Little drones they play with," almost like "Ike and George Patton" when the two were testing out new tank technology between the first and second World War. "Who's doing that now?" Miller's point was that there's always some new technology to disrupt the battlefield. Right now that's clearly drones. Which of our senior strategic leaders are experimenting, getting hands on, developing a fingertip feel for this new warfighting tech? It's a suggestion Grant would endorse in his view that each war is different.

So much of this kind of learning is beyond anything you can put your finger on. It begins with an independence of mind. It's hard to pin down because it's in the air and intangible. "This is the stuff that nobody tells you to do," Rear Admiral Studeman said, "It's the stuff that your instinct tells you that you should be doing."

But to a strategic leader, it's also totally transparent. All in the open for everyone to see; "An officer's always on parade," as General Neller put it.

In one more way we can spot a lesson in strategic leadership from Grant's judgment—his empathy for others.

In this campaign, and before, Grant displayed a human empathy that likely augmented his strategic leadership. After the opening days of the campaign in the Battle of the Wilderness, Grant wept over the knowledge that finishing the war would mean the end of so many lives, and that he would be the one driving that tragic result. One staff officer describing the incident wrote, "When proper measures had been taken, Grant went into his tent, threw himself face down upon his cot, and gave way to the greatest emotion." The officer asserted he had "never before seen [Grant] so deeply moved" and that "nothing could be more certain than that he was stirred to the very depths of his soul." Writing separately, Charles Adams Jr. confirmed that he "never saw a man so agitated in my life." And, just like that, it passed, and shortly thereafter, another staff officer wrote, "I looked in his tent, and found him sleeping as soundly and as peacefully as an infant."[10]

This burst of empathy was not the only time Grant was moved to tears during a Civil War campaign. His son Frederick recalled in a post-war memoir a similar occurrence during the Vicksburg campaign in 1863:

> A small boy, with blood streaming from a wound in his leg, came running to where father and [William T.] Sherman stood, and reported that his regiment was out of ammunition. Sherman was directing some attention to be paid to his wound, when the little fellow, finding himself fainting from loss of blood, gasped out, "Calibre 56," as he was carried off to the rear. At this moment I observed that my father's eyes were filled with tears.[11]

During the 1864 campaign itself, Grant showed another sort of compassion, for animals, when he saw a Union worker flogging some horses. Grant called the man a "scoundrel," and had him tied to a tree for six hours for "brutality."[12]

There is also documented evidence that the other two strategic leaders—Washington and Eisenhower—shed tears during their respective campaigns. For George Washington, it happened on November 16, 1776, as he watched helplessly while Fort Washington fell to the British.[13] Dwight D. Eisenhower broke down on June 5, 1944, as he watched paratroopers board planes bound for Normandy. He wept again years later when reunited with a group of those same airborne veterans in 1952.[14]

Some may dismiss these moments as brief signs of emotion in dark times. But they may also reveal something deeper: a genuine sense of empathy. These men, despite the burden of command, truly understood the stakes and cared for the soldiers they led.

Empathy—the ability to understand others—matters in strategic leadership.[15] It helps a supreme commander relate not only to troops but also to political leaders, allies, and even enemies. Historian Hew Strachan once wrote that the biggest challenge in war is often the connection between "statesmen and soldiers"—the intersection of political and military goals.[16] Empathy helps bridge that gap.

A commander who naturally understands people may better grasp what political leaders want and need. That understanding allows the commander to keep military actions aligned with political strategy. Sometimes, empathy allows a commander to see what others cannot and steer the war effort in a smarter direction—or, in certain cases, lead in a direction unconsidered by distant political leadership that better serves a country's strategic ends. Such empathy might also help a supreme commander to better understand the enemy's mind.[17]

Empathy also helps knit alliances together. Strategic leaders must manage egos, rivalries, and conflicting priorities within their own coalitions. The "sensible application of superior resources," as one strategist put it, only works if the commander can bring everyone together behind a single plan.[18] That requires emotional intelligence.

On a broader level, the scholar Amy Chua has argued that every global power that has achieved dominance did so by being relatively tolerant. Great powers, she's written, find ways to "motivate the world's best and brightest" regardless of background or identity.[19] They succeed by "gluing" people together in a shared cause.[20] In wartime, Washington, Grant, and Eisenhower acted as that "glue," binding different groups into one effective force. With Washington, it was his respect for the Continental Congress's role; with Grant, his deference to Lincoln's political needs in an election year so tied to the war effort; and with Eisenhower, as we'll see, his courteous interplay at the highest levels of American and Allied governments.

Empathy keeps a supreme commander alert—listening, watching, and learning. It makes them open to the best ideas, wherever those ideas come from, and helps them understand both friend and foe.

And it works. Grant stopped Robert E. Lee's army, held it in place, supported victories by other Union generals, and helped bring the Union war effort together. In less than a year, his strategic leadership helped win the war.[21]

Grant's record is hard to ignore. He led successful campaigns that forced three major Confederate armies to surrender: at Fort Donelson in 1862, Vicksburg in 1863, and Appomattox in 1865.[22] Grant was, above all, effective, superior—and victorious.

Part IV

HOW EISENHOWER WON

Chapter 9

CHALLENGE: EISENHOWER AND HITLER, 1944

It would be difficult to conceive of a more soul-racking problem.
—Dwight D. Eisenhower

The day before D-Day, General Dwight Eisenhower wrote a short, grim message in case the invasion failed (and even misdated it in his nervousness):

Our landings in the Cherbourg-Havre area have failed to gain a satisfactory foothold and I have withdrawn the troops. My decision to attack at this time and place was based upon the best information available. The troops, the air and the Navy did all that Bravery and devotion to duty could do. If any blame or fault attaches to the attempt it is mine alone.[1]

Earlier that day, Eisenhower said quietly to his driver, "I hope to God I know what I'm doing."[2]

Eleven months later, when the war in Europe ended, Eisenhower simply wrote, "The mission of this Allied Force was fulfilled at 0241, local time, May 7th, 1945. Signed Eisenhower."[3] Simple. Conclusive. Maybe even confidently written.

The sharp difference between that earlier note and his later victory message raises questions. How did the Allies win? Why was Eisenhower so worried in June 1944 and then so calm by May 1945? What made this campaign succeed?

"There are many parallels," historian Jean Smith noted when comparing Ulysses S. Grant and Dwight D. Eisenhower. Both were professional soldiers educated at West Point. Both were victorious in enormous wars. Both were elected president twice and left office popular.[4]

Eisenhower's strategic success was as final to the Nazis as Grant's had been to the Confederates. Both men faced major challenges as strategic leaders in wars that shaped history.

The campaign itself was enormous. As Supreme Allied Commander Europe, Eisenhower directed 4.5 million American troops and 1 million Allied soldiers in total. He oversaw 91 divisions, 28,000 aircraft, 470,000 vehicles, and 18 million tons of supplies.[5] Historian Max Hastings noted that about 2.9 million Allied troops fought in the immediate area of Normandy alone.[6]

This was modern, industrial, global war. The Allies planned a complex invasion using land, sea, and air forces. They fought as a coalition, working through disagreements among different nations.[7] One historian called the invasion "easily the largest and most complicated multinational, tri-service amphibious landings in the history of mankind."[8]

The Nazis had advantages. They were defending territory, with years to prepare, and initially had a significant numerical edge at the beach.

They also had psychological weapons—advanced rocket and missile technology—that unsettled the Allies.[9] There were solid reasons to doubt the invasion would succeed.

By 1944, the Nazis were stretched thin. On the Eastern Front, Soviet forces had taken the Crimean peninsula, Ukraine, and land near Estonia, using up Nazi military strength. Of the Nazis' 298 total divisions in the war at the time, 193 were in the East, 28 in Italy, 18 in Scandinavia, and 59 in France, Belgium, and the Netherlands. These 59 divisions formed the Atlantic Wall the Allies needed to break through.[10]

The Allies were similarly tied down in other theaters. In the Pacific, the United States faced Japan with about 30 Army divisions and all six Marine divisions. That meant fewer troops were available for Europe.[11] The same was true for the Nazis, which kept large forces fighting the Soviets—like the 28 Nazi divisions the Soviets ground down in 1944's Operation Bagration.[12] For both the Allied and Axis powers, global war made local resources scarce—but each still had enough to fight for victory in France.

Eisenhower commanded all Allied forces in this campaign. Yet some of his contemporaries were critical of him. British General Bernard Montgomery said Eisenhower "doesn't know the difference between Christmas and Easter" when it came to war. Fellow General Alan Brooke wrote in his diary that Eisenhower was "no real director of thought, plans, energy, or direction," and saw him only as a good coordinator and team player, not a real commander.[13]

This view was not uncommon. Critics often praise Eisenhower's people skills but dismiss his strategic acumen. One historian said Eisenhower's biggest contribution to D-Day was simply his "historic decision to launch" despite bad weather—making it sound like that was his sole contribution.[14] Other historians downplay the role of Eisenhower's strategic leadership altogether. Richard Overy, in *Why the Allies Won*, wrote that the two biggest reasons for Allied success in France were airpower and deception.[15] Paul Kennedy, in *Engineers of Victory*, pointed to "command of the air, command of the sea," as well as deception, intelligence, and weather.[16] These arguments suggest the tools of war mattered more than the leaders using them.

But those assessments miss a key question: *How* should such tools be used? Airpower, for example—should it strike French railways over a long lead-up to invasion, focus on German cities, or hit the immediate areas around the beaches just before landing? Should Nazi defenses be placed right on the shore or farther inland as a mobile force? In the way Overy and Kennedy present their cases, these issues are brushed aside. Such a view ignores the real debates within the Allied high command. These weren't just technical questions—they were strategic ones. Eisenhower made those hard decisions, and to leave them out is to ignore his central role.

This chapter focuses on those kinds of judgments. Historian Ian Kershaw has written, "A decision implies there were choices to be made, alternatives available . . . There was no inexorable path to be followed."[17]

THE PATH TO NORMANDY

In the lead-up to Normandy, top Allied leaders strongly disagreed with the cross-channel invasion. In February 1944, British Prime Minister Winston Churchill asked, "Why are we trying to do this?"[18] Two months later, Churchill told an American general that he would have waited to recover Norway, taken some Aegean islands, and brought Turkey into the war—all before the attempted invasion of France.[19]

On the eve of the landings, General Brooke wrote, "I am very uneasy about the whole operation. At the best, it will come very far short of the expectations . . . At its worst, it may well be the most ghastly disaster of the war."[20]

Despite disagreements, one individual made all the final calls: Dwight D. Eisenhower.

Eisenhower came from a line of Quakers, with a distant ancestor who had fought with Washington in 1776. He graduated from West Point in 1915.[21] A good athlete, he was nearly six feet tall, and weighed 190 pounds during his football-playing days.[22] Though he ranked 61st in a class of 164, friends believed he could've ranked much higher if not for his many extracurriculars. "Everyone was his friend," one recalled.[23]

His early career was broad and varied. He worked on tank doctrine, served in Panama and the Philippines, and worked with the post–World War I American Battle Monuments Commission in France.[24] Though stuck at the rank of major for 16 years, his rise in World War II was stunning: from lieutenant colonel to five-star general in just 42 months.[25]

On March 9, 1942, Eisenhower became chief of the Army's War Plans Division.[26] Soon after, the US began planning BOLERO, the buildup for a cross-channel attack. Two early versions were considered: SLEDGEHAMMER (a possible 1942 diversion if the Soviets were in trouble) and ROUNDUP (the main attack envisioned for 1943). At the same time, Eisenhower wrote to General George Marshall that Germany should be the first target, attacked through Western Europe.[27]

From the beginning, the Allies agreed there had to be one commander for major operations. General Brooke advised, "There should always be a Supreme Commander in a theatre where active operations are in progress."[28] Eisenhower was promoted to general and, on June 24, 1942, made commander of the European Theater of Operations US Army (ETOUSA).

Though he had never commanded troops in combat or led above a battalion, he was chosen to lead the invasion of North Africa.[29]

While Eisenhower prepared in North Africa, the Allies met at Casablanca in January 1943 and created a planning group for the later invasion of France.[30] They chose British Lieutenant General Frederick Morgan as Chief of Staff to the Supreme Allied Commander (COSSAC).[31] Morgan and his team picked the broad location for the landings and outlined the mission.[32] The detailed plans would be finalized later by the (yet to be selected) Supreme Commander.

That Supreme Commander was announced on December 24, 1943 (following a decision at the Tehran Conference): Eisenhower would lead the Normandy invasion.[33]

His chief of staff later recalled, "As Supreme Commander, General Eisenhower was in direct command of the forces dedicated to the conquest of Hitler's armies." The Allies placed full "responsibility" on Eisenhower and gave him the authority to decide how to defeat Nazi Germany in the West.[34]

Not only did Eisenhower receive authority to command the invasion, but with General George Marshall's support, he also selected nearly all the senior military commanders in the European Theater.[35] Moreover, in a list of the 22 documented instances when President Franklin D. Roosevelt overruled military commanders, not once did Roosevelt reverse a decision made by Eisenhower.[36] Even in a democratic alliance where many actors held influence, Eisenhower functioned as a true supreme commander and strategic leader.

His opposite was Adolf Hitler. In February 1938, Hitler named himself "Supreme Commander of the Armed Forces" and treated this title seriously. He personally made decisions about Nazi strategy and military operations and refused to share that power with others.[37]

Hitler held total authority over Germany's military. He sometimes discussed strategic matters with senior officers, but Hitler always made the final call. Of 650 major Nazi wartime orders, 578 were issued by Hitler himself.[38]

Some may argue that comparing Eisenhower, a military officer, to Hitler, a political dictator, is inappropriate. Hitler ruled a country (and more), while Eisenhower commanded a theater of war and answered to higher authorities. But wartime leaders are rarely identical. If exact symmetry were a requirement, we could never study many of history's opposing commanders side by side.

Instead, we use a more flexible definition. A "supreme commander" or "executive military strategist," as Colin Gray put it, is someone responsible for making strategic decisions to shape the outcome of a conflict. As Gray wrote, Hitler could act as both "general" and "grand strategist," overseeing the military and the broader political goals of war.[39] So while the two were not equals in title or role, Hitler was Eisenhower's decision-making adversary in the war for Western Europe.

Some critics go further and argue Hitler was insane or incompetent, using his immoral actions to discredit any serious discussion of his military acumen. Yet this view ignores the fact that Hitler achieved early military success and built a powerful war machine. As historian Edward Meade Earle wrote in 1943, "Hitler deserves credit for astute conduct of the war."[40] Military theorist Basil Liddell Hart added that "Hitler had a natural flair for strategy and tactics."[41] Besides, strategic leadership is a morally neutral tool, like a knife. It can be used for good (a scalpel in a surgeon's hands) or ill (a weapon in a murderer's hands).

Hitler had clear strategic goals. He wanted to establish a

"Thousand-Year Reich." In a 1942 speech, he described the war as an epic battle "which usher[s] in a new millennium."[42] His aim was to create living space—*Lebensraum*—for his chosen people through the conquest of Europe, including Russia and beyond.[43]

More narrowly, Hitler provided detailed instructions for defending occupied France in his "Führer Directive Number 51," issued November 3, 1943. He declared that France would be where "the decisive landing battles will be fought."[44] He predicted that the Allies would land on the Normandy coast. Later, in December 1943, he said, "There's no doubt that the attack in the West will come in the spring."[45] Hitler understood that a successful Allied invasion could upend the Western Front.

Hitler also hoped the 1944 US presidential election would finish with Roosevelt's defeat, ending America's war effort.[46] So while his long-term plan was global domination, his goal in 1944 was to repel the Allies.

The American strategy was based on several key ideas. Far from the battlefield, the United States would act as the "Arsenal of Democracy," relying on logistics, firepower, and expeditionary forces. The Americans knew they could not win alone, so they built a strong alliance with the British and a necessary partnership with the Soviets. They prioritized defeating Germany before turning fully to Japan.[47]

In this context, Eisenhower received official orders on February 12, 1944, to lead Operation OVERLORD. His chief of staff noted the "broad latitude given to the commander."[48] Eisenhower's 30-word guidance was clear: "You will enter the continent of Europe and, in conjunction with the other united nations, undertake operations aimed at the heart of Germany and the destruction of her armed forces."[49]

Eisenhower later wrote that his aim was "to bring all our strength against [the adversary], all of it mobile, and all of it contributing directly to the complete annihilation of [Germany's] field forces."[50]

To achieve this, the Allies required a continental foothold. In January 1944, Eisenhower met with General Bernard Montgomery in London to discuss the main effort (OVERLORD) and the supporting effort (ANVIL). One of the biggest early concerns was the size of the landing force. Eisenhower thought the existing plan—three divisions landing on the beach, with two in reserve—was too small. He believed the plan failed to emphasize the importance of capturing ports and building up supplies quickly.[51]

Montgomery agreed. In his report to Prime Minister Churchill, Montgomery called the original plan "impracticable" and "confied [*sic*] to too small an area." He believed the landings needed to happen "on the widest possible front."[52]

This meeting led to a January 23, 1944, message from Eisenhower to the Allied Chiefs of Staff, summarizing key concerns:

We are convinced . . . this operation marks the crisis of the European war. Every obstacle must be overcome, every inconvenience suffered and every risk run to ensure that our blow is decisive. We cannot afford to fail . . .

To ensure success we consider it essential to increase the assault force to five divisions . . .

Our reasons for this view are that an operation of this type must be designed to obtain an adequate bridgehead quickly and to retain the initiative . . . It will be essential to extend the front to give us a greater opportunity of finding a weak spot through which to exploit success . . .

I regard "ANVIL" as an important contribution to "OVERLORD" . . . "OVERLORD" and "ANVIL" must be viewed as one whole. If sufficient forces could be made available the ideal would be a five divisional "OVERLORD" and a three divisional "ANVIL" or, at worst, a two divisional "ANVIL."[53]

In this cable, Eisenhower discusses the main effort (OVERLORD) and a secondary landing for mostly supply purposes (ANVIL). In it we see Eisenhower making high-level judgments about troop strength, coordination, and risk—core functions of strategic leadership.

Meanwhile, the Nazis worked to strengthen the Atlantic Wall to repel the invasion. The 1940 campaigns expanded their occupied coastline to 3,500 miles. Vice Admiral Friedrich Ruge, a key naval advisor, noted that earlier Allied raids had taught the Nazis to expect attacks not on major ports but on beaches, followed by moves inland.[54]

Field Marshal Gerd von Rundstedt, Nazi commander in the West, believed the Allies would land sometime after March at the shortest point between Britain and France (at Pas de Calais).[55] In an October 1943 memo, he also listed Normandy and Brittany as likely targets. Rundstedt believed Germany could win either by defending the coast directly or by using large mobile reserves to push the Allies back into the sea.[56]

Around this time, Hitler issued Führer Directive 51, a document that shaped Nazi strategy. Hitler wrote, "The threat from the East remains, but an even greater danger looms in the West: the Anglo-American landing!"

He believed that even if the Soviets took large parts of Eastern Europe, Germany could survive. But if the Western Allies broke through in France, it would be fatal. Hitler concluded, "I can no longer justify the further weakening of the West in favor of other theaters of war. I have therefore decided to strengthen the defenses in the West."

He ordered more troops, more materials, faster construction of coastal fortifications. Hitler demanded that the Allies "must be hit by the full fury of our counterattack" and insisted on having trained reserves ready to prevent any expansion of a beachhead.[57]

In November 1943, after reading Rundstedt's report, Hitler sent Field Marshal Erwin Rommel and his full staff (over 200 officers) to assess how best to stop the invasion. Rommel studied the challenge carefully and was given command over Army Group B, responsible for defending the Netherlands, and Pas de Calais and Normandy in France. This structure placed Rommel under Rundstedt but gave him direct control over much of the defensive line.[58]

By both word (in Directive 51) and action (sending Rommel), Hitler showed that he saw France—and particularly the Normandy area—as the war's critical theater in 1944.

COULD THE NAZIS HAVE WON EITHER THIS CAMPAIGN OR THE WAR?

Did Hitler still have a real chance to win in 1944? Could the Nazis have turned the tide in Normandy and continued toward their larger goals in the war?

Victory for the Allies at Normandy wasn't guaranteed. Even with overwhelming airpower—11,590 Allied aircraft to just 319 Nazi planes—the first wave of the American air bombardment failed to kill a single Nazi defender on Omaha Beach. German bunkers made of reinforced concrete withstood the attack. For ground forces, the situation was just as difficult. American soldiers carried packs weighing around 75 pounds.[59] Many drowned as they waded from the landing craft to the shore. Supply lines were fragile, and setting up a steady flow of equipment from beaches was extremely hard. All this made failure possible.

Historians have studied what might have happened if the invasion had failed.[60] Some even speculated that the atomic bomb—later dropped on Japan—might have been used in Europe instead.

Historian Stephen Ambrose wrote that Hitler "could have used the D-Day failure to split the strange alliance of West and East."[61] Ambrose also suggested that Nazi propaganda might have convinced Stalin that the United Kingdom and United States would bleed the Soviets dry, which could have restarted the earlier Nazi–Soviet partnership.

Historian Dennis Showalter explored another scenario. If Rommel's defenses at the Atlantic Wall had held the Allies off, the Nazis might have forced a negotiated peace.[62] British strategist Basil Liddell Hart wrote in *The Daily Mail* in 1943 that "by inflicting a disastrous repulse on its would-be invaders," Germany might have forced the Allies to "modify their demand for Germany's unconditional surrender."[63]

There had long been fears that Stalin might strike a separate deal with Hitler. Rumors swirled for years about Soviet diplomats in Sweden making peace overtures to the Nazis.[64]

Historian Samuel Eliot Morison raised another concern, continuing missile attacks on London:

If we had not invaded Northern Europe in the summer of 1944, London would have been laid flat by the V-1 bombs and V-2 rockets . . . Could [the British] . . . have withstood an accelerated and intensified V-2 offensive?[65]

Failure at Normandy would have had two devastating effects for the Allies. First, politically, it might have pushed Stalin into another deal with Hitler.[66] Second, strategically, the continued missile attack on

Britain might have crushed public morale and forced political leaders to rethink the war.

The Allied leaders knew how much was riding on the invasion. Eisenhower certainly understood the stakes. So did Hitler, who said in December 1943, "If they attack in the West, [then] this attack will decide the war."[67]

Both sides saw the Normandy campaign as decisive. And while the Allies did win, it was far from certain. Hitler had real pathways to success. A failure by the Allies could have led to a political crisis, a renewed Nazi–Soviet pact, and a continued rocket and missile campaign that might have changed the course of history.

Chapter 10

CHOICES AND CLASHES: EISENHOWER AND HITLER, 1944

The eyes of the world are upon you. The hopes and prayers
of liberty-loving people everywhere march with you.
—Dwight D. Eisenhower (June 6, 1944)

HOW SHOULD EISENHOWER USE AIRPOWER? HOW SHOULD HITLER DEFEND?

"Unless the matter is settled at once I will request relief from this Command," wrote General Eisenhower, taking a stand on March 22, 1944, just months into his role as Supreme Commander.[1]

Why was Eisenhower ready to resign? It wasn't personal pride. It was a deep strategic disagreement with heavy consequences. The central issue was how to best use airpower to support the Normandy invasion.

When General Eisenhower arrived to take command in January 1944, he wrote to US Army Air Force General Carl Spaatz that Spaatz's headquarters would now operate alongside British Bomber Command "under [the] general direction of the Supreme Commander."[2] But within a few months, both Spaatz and British Bomber Command resisted Eisenhower's plans for how airpower should support the invasion, and both opposed "submitting to Eisenhower's control." British Royal Air Force leaders, including the chief of the Air Staff and Prime Minister Winston Churchill, also supported keeping airpower independent from Eisenhower's authority.[3]

Tensions grew so severe that on March 22, 1944, Eisenhower wrote of the "air problem" and explained that "the British had a great fear that the American idea was to seize all the air in Great Britain and apply it very locally in preparation of OVERLORD."

Eisenhower believed the Allies needed to disable France's railways to stop the Germans from quickly sending reinforcements to the beaches.[4] As Eisenhower's aide Harry Butcher put it on March 27, 1944, the question was "whether strategic bombers on oil or transportation [were] the best means of helping OVERLORD," which was "a question for Ike to determine."[5]

Eisenhower considered two options. The first was interdiction: targeted, short-term bombing just before D-Day to cut train lines, destroy bridges, and hit key rail hubs.[6] The second, proposed by Air Marshal Trafford Leigh-Mallory, was the "Transportation Plan," a longer campaign to wear down the entire French rail system, including train tracks, repair shops, and rolling stock, even reaching into Belgium.[7]

Interdiction focused on sharp, last-minute strikes. The Transportation Plan called for a sustained effort to break the rail system before the invasion. Leigh-Mallory believed interdiction depended too much on good weather, which couldn't be guaranteed. A study on February 12, 1944, by the American Expeditionary Air Forces (AEAF), supported the Transportation Plan, showing that two-thirds of French rail traffic was German military. That meant bombing the system would directly harm the Nazi war effort. But this long-term bombing required strategic bombers, pulling them away from deep strikes against Germany's oil supply and war factories.[8]

On February 15, 1944, General Spaatz and British Air Chief Marshal Arthur Harris argued against the Transportation Plan. Spaatz said it would take bombers away from more important missions. Harris agreed and added that the plan wrongly assumed interdiction wouldn't work. Their view was shared by many British leaders: Churchill, General Alan Brooke, Air Chief Marshal Charles Portal, the Joint Intelligence Committee, and the Ministry of Economic Warfare. They believed rail interdiction would be more effective and less damaging to the French people. A study by US Embassy rail experts in London claimed only one-fifth of French rail was used by the Germans—far less than the two-thirds estimate in the AEAF report. (Postwar analysis would later show the real figure was about one-third.)[9] The figure assessed the degree to which the bombing would likely harm French civilians instead of the Nazi defenders.

Spaatz proposed a different idea on March 5, 1944: the "Plan for the Completion of the Combined Bomber Offensive." It aimed to destroy Germany's oil supply. He said that just 14 plants produced 80% of Germany's synthetic oil. If bombers hit those, the effect would be "catastrophic." Germany, he said, could afford to lose 14 rail centers more easily than those 14 oil plants.[10]

Leigh-Mallory responded by emphasizing the risk of waiting. If air attacks were saved for the last minute, bad weather might ruin everything. Eventually, Harris changed his position and supported the Transportation Plan. He may have been persuaded by Deputy Supreme Commander Air Chief Marshal Arthur Tedder, who argued that oil targets were too far away to affect the invasion in time, while the rail network could be hit soon enough to make a difference.[11]

So Eisenhower made his decision. On March 25, 1944, at an Allied conference, he announced for the Transportation Plan. He believed it offered the best support to secure the invasion's beachhead. On April 14, Eisenhower ordered the plan to commence.[12]

He explained his reasoning in a letter to Churchill on April 5, 1944:

> After long study . . . we decided that the only preparatory field in which our air force could be profitably employed . . . was against the enemy's transportation system…
>
> I and my military advisors have become convinced that the bombing of these centers will increase our chances for success in the critical battle.
>
> The French people are now slaves. Only a successful OVERLORD can free them . . .
>
> While we must do everything possible to avoid loss of life among our friends, I think it would be sheer folly to abstain from doing anything that can increase . . . our chances for success in OVERLORD.
>
> [The] French people would accept these bombings as a necessary sacrifice incident to [the Germans'] earlier defeat.[13]

The commander of the Free French Forces initially objected, but changed his mind after a full briefing. Eisenhower's chief of staff noted, of the French general's response, "'C'est la guerre' was never used with deeper feeling."[14]

Still, British resistance continued. On April 29, 1944, Eisenhower wrote to General Marshall, "The British Government has been trying to induce me to change my bombing program . . . I have stuck to my guns because there is no other way."[15]

These were the tough trade-offs between military effectiveness and political compromise, which can be seen in Eisenhower's note to Prime Minister Churchill on May 2, 1944:

I have . . . realized the political considerations arising from . . . civilian casualties...

I directed that the remaining Railway targets involving the greatest risk . . . be attacked at a later stage . . .

Although this postponement . . . affects the full efficacy of the Plan . . .

I must point out that casualties . . . are inherent in any plan for the full use of Air power . . .

He went on to explain that the mission wasn't to stop all German troop movement, but to delay reinforcements long enough for the Allies to establish a secure foothold.[16] He closed with a warning:

I have modified my plan as far as possible without vitiating its value . . .

If [political concerns] limit the Operations [any more], such a modification would emasculate the whole plan . . .

The OVERLORD concept was based on the assumption that our overwhelming Air power would be able to prepare the way for the assault. If its hands are to be tied, the perils of an already hazardous undertaking will be greatly enhanced.[17]

Eisenhower made a strategic decision after considering all options and political pressures. One historian later noted that, as a result of the aerial bombardment, "by June 6, 1944, French rail traffic was a mere 30 percent what it had been in January; by early July, it was only 10 percent."[18] And while early estimates feared up to 160,000 civilian casualties would result from the Transportation Plan, the final figure was around 10,000.[19] While tragic, it was far less than predicted. Eisenhower had weighed military necessity against political cost—and made a hard, effective decision.

When Hitler received the first report of the Allied landings on June 6, 1944, he said, "I am glad that the Anglo-Americans have finally decided to land in France, and exactly where they were expected. Now we know where we are."[20] Until that moment, the Nazis hadn't known exactly when or where the invasion would happen.[21] Uncertainty made preparation difficult.

Germany's territorial gains in 1940 created a large coastline to defend.[22] This was both an advantage and a burden. As historian Dennis Showalter explained:

> The Fifteenth Army in the Pas de Calais sector eventually grew to a strength of 18 infantry and two panzer divisions, responsible for about 340 miles of coastline. The Seventh Army, responsible for Normandy and Brittany, had 14 infantry divisions and a single panzer division. It was responsible for 995 miles of coast. One of its divisions had a defensive sector of 62 miles; another was expected to secure no fewer than 167 miles.[23]

With so much ground to cover, German leaders disagreed about how best to respond to an invasion. In March 1942, Field Marshal Rundstedt became commander of Nazi forces in France and the western territories.

Later, to highlight the importance of the region, Hitler placed Field Marshal Rommel in charge of Army Group B, which oversaw the 15th and 7th Armies—including those defending Normandy.[24] Both commands were under Rundstedt, yet Rommel was given wide authority.

Rommel could now command Panzer Group West forces in his area and recommend their assignments directly to Rundstedt, bypassing another general, Leo Geyr von Schweppenburg. This overlap in authority created friction among senior leaders that Hitler had to mediate.[25]

Rommel believed the best chance of stopping the invasion was to strike at the beaches. He wanted to use small, fast-moving Nazi units to crush the Allies before they could get established. Rommel worried that once the Allies had a foothold, it would be too late.[26]

Rommel's ideas on the defense were not just opposed by Rundstedt, but also General von Schweppenburg, who in July 1943 was given command of another major unit in the same area. He thought Germany should hold its armored forces farther back and wait to launch large counterattacks after identifying the main invasion site. Rundstedt supported this view. But Rommel warned that Allied airpower would make it nearly impossible for big German units to get to the beach quickly. In his view, trying to counterattack from deep inland would take too long and fail.[27]

In the end, Hitler made a compromise that satisfied no one. He had 10 mechanized divisions to spend as a reserve. He sent three south to guard against a possible Allied landing there, leaving seven for the defense of northern France's coastline. Instead of keeping them together, Hitler split them up: Three went under Rommel's direct control in Army Group B, while the other four stayed under Panzer Group West (which could only be released by Hitler himself).

This decision ensured the Nazi counterattack would be too weak and too slow. Historian Paul Kennedy has argued that if four panzer divisions had been placed closer to Normandy and given quicker release authority, they might have changed the outcome.[28] But Hitler's indecision between Rommel and Rundstedt prevented that.[29]

Many German officers later criticized the failed command structure. Vice Admiral Friedrich Ruge said there was "no uniform defence plan."[30] General Gunther Blumentritt, Rundstedt's Chief of Staff, said the "chain of command was very complicated and muddled." He added that when the invasion came on June 6, 1944, "freedom of action . . . was impossible."[31] Both Rommel and Rundstedt requested permission to use the mechanized reserve. Both were denied.[32] Ruge concluded the defense failed because of the "lack of a single, clear-cut plan, carried out under the responsibility of a single, experienced commander."[33]

HOW SHOULD EISENHOWER USE AIRBORNE DROPS? HOW SHOULD HITLER USE V-WEAPONS?

Early in the planning for the invasion of France, the Combined Chiefs of Staff provided COSSAC planners two American airborne divisions.[34] But deciding where to drop them became a major issue. Two key leaders disagreed: British Air Chief Marshal Trafford Leigh-Mallory and American General George Marshall.

On February 10, 1944, Marshall wrote to Eisenhower, "Up to the present time I have not felt that we have properly exploited air power as regards its combination with ground troops."[35]

Marshall was originally considered for overall command of the invasion, so his opinion likely carried weight with Eisenhower. Marshall felt so strongly about this suggestion that he tasked three of his own staff officers to create options for airborne drops. Of the three, Marshall favored "Plan C":

> The area generally south of Evreux [200km inland from Normandy; 100km to Paris] . . . has been selected because of four excellent airfields . . . It would directly threaten the crossings of the Seine as well as the city of Paris . . . In effect, we would be opening another front in France and your build-up would be tremendously increased.[36]

Marshall knew it was bold and risky:

> The trouble with this plan is that we have never done anything like this before . . . Therefore I should like you to give these young men an opportunity to present the matter to you personally before your Staff tears it to ribbons.[37]

Marshall and US Army Air Corps General Hap Arnold both supported the plan. But Eisenhower disagreed. He thought dropping troops so far inland—two-thirds of the way to Paris—was too dangerous.[38]

Nine days later, Eisenhower replied:

> I agree thoroughly with the conception but disagree with the timing . . . the time for mass vertical envelopment is after the beach-head has been gained . . . [Our first priority] is for the Expeditionary Force to gain a firm and solid footing on the Continent and to secure at least one really good sheltered harbor.[39]

Eisenhower focused on breaking through the beach defenses and holding ground. He continued that he worried that "any significant part of our forces . . . [would become] isolated and defeated in detail."[40]

Eisenhower believed the airborne units should directly support the beach landings, not operate independently deep inland. He feared isolated units could be surrounded and destroyed by mobile German forces.

A week before D-Day, Eisenhower faced more doubts. His aide, Navy Captain Harry Butcher, wrote on May 30, 1944, that Eisenhower had "a tough one today" because Leigh-Mallory "has 'gone on record' . . . emphasizing his fear of colossal losses in the American paratroop operation."[41]

On May 22, Eisenhower himself had written in his diary about the challenge: "We have run into a great deal of difficulty because of the almost universal coverage of the European continent by strong flak," which meant "the Eighty-second Airborne Division will have a most sticky time of it."[42]

Leigh-Mallory warned in a letter: "If the success of the seaborne assault . . . depends on the airborne, it will be seriously prejudiced."[43]

Eisenhower later recalled Leigh-Mallory predicted up to 70% losses in the American airborne forces, making them useless in battle.[44] His chief of staff remembered the estimate as even worse: 75% to 80%.[45]

Eisenhower replied to Leigh-Mallory:

> You are quite right . . . as to the hazards involved . . . However, a strong airborne attack in the region indicated is essential to the whole operation and it must go on . . . There is nothing for it but for you, the Army Commander, and the Troop Carrier Commander to work out . . . every single thing that may diminish

these hazards . . . I am . . . hopeful that our percentage losses will not approximate your estimates.[46]

This was one of Eisenhower's hardest decisions. In *Crusade in Europe*, written after the war, he reflected deeply:

Later, on May 30, [Leigh-Mallory] came to me to protest once more against what he termed the "futile slaughter" of two fine divisions . . . he estimated . . . seventy per cent losses in glider strength and at least fifty per cent in paratroop strength before the airborne troops could land . . . Consequently the divisions would have no remaining tactical power.[47]

Eisenhower knew Leigh-Mallory was sincere, and wrote:

It would be difficult to conceive of a more soul-racking problem . . . If my technical expert was correct, then the planned operation was worse than stubborn folly . . . I would carry to my grave the unbearable burden of . . . the stupid, blind sacrifice of thousands.[48]

Eisenhower explained how he reached his final decision:

If I should cancel the airborne operation, then I had either to cancel the attack on Utah Beach or . . . condemn the assaulting forces there to even greater probability of disaster . . . To abandon it really meant to abandon a plan in which I had held explicit confidence for more than two years.[49]

He also questioned the predictions:

Leigh-Mallory's estimate was just an estimate, nothing more . . .
our experience in Sicily and Italy did not, by any means, support
his degree of pessimism.[50]

In the end, Eisenhower made the call: "I telephoned [Leigh-Mallory]
that the attack would go as planned and that I would confirm this at once
in writing."[51]

Though the airborne drops were scattered, they succeeded in disrupting the Nazi counterattack and helped support the landings.[52] Eisenhower later reported that actual airborne casualties were around 8%—far lower than feared.[53] Once the beachhead was secure, Leigh-Mallory called Eisenhower to express "his delight and to express his regret that he had found it necessary to add to my personal burdens during the final tense days before D-Day."[54]

While Eisenhower was managing airborne operations in preparation for D-Day, Adolf Hitler oversaw the development of secret weapons meant to terrorize the Allies and possibly turn the tide of the war. These were the so-called V-weapons ("V" standing for *Vergeltungswaffe*—German for "vengeance weapon"). V-weapons included the V-1 flying bomb and the V-2 rocket. On July 28, 1943, having absorbed the British bombing of Hamburg, Germany, Hitler was furious and quickly approved V-weapon deployment in France. While the German Army had sponsored a ballistic missile program in the 1930s, it was stepped up during World War II.[55]

Hitler laid out his thinking on the V-weapons at a July 1943 military conference:

The English will only stop when their towns are destroyed, nothing else will do it . . . I can only win the war by destroying more on the enemy's side than he does on ours—by inflicting on his the horror of war.[56]

By 1944, the Nazi conventional military strength was weakening. Hitler hoped new technology could change the course of the war. In a sense, the V-weapons represented the Nazi regime's last major attempt to force political collapse on its enemies. According to historian Steven Zaloga, Hitler spent about $3 billion on the V-weapons, far more even than the US atomic bomb program.[57]

The first deployed was the V-1, an early type of cruise missile. It was launched from static ramps in occupied France, aimed primarily at London. Though slow enough to be heard coming, the V-1 could still cause widespread damage. The V-1's range was roughly 130 miles.

The V-1 campaign began shortly after the D-Day landings. In mid-June 1944, London came under heavy bombardment as hundreds of V-1s were launched from sites in northern France.[58] British civilians soon called them "buzz bombs" or "doodlebugs" due to the distinctive sound of the engine. When the engine cut out, people knew the bomb was soon to fall.[59]

The V-2 was "ground-breaking rocket technology," as historian Andrew Roberts has written. The V-2 was a "supersonic ballistic missile" that flew at 3,600 mph, carried a one-ton warhead, and was "by far the biggest weapon of its kind." The V-2 was "launched from an upright position from vehicles that simply drove off after firing," so "it did not even have launch-pad installations . . . that the Allies could bomb and overrun." The V-2's first combat strike was on "a suburb of Paris on September 8, 1944; the second struck London . . . hours later."[60]

In all, from June 13, 1944, to April 1945, as Steven Zaloga has written, the "German missile campaign against British and Belgian cities in 1944–45 was the first large-scale use of guided missiles in history with some 23,172 V-1 and 3,172 V-2 missiles launched."[61] Damage was significant:

> [M]ore than 24,000 Britons were casualties of the Fuehrer's vicious "secret weapon," with 5,475 of them dying . . . At one point during the initial assault in July and August 1944 10,000 homes were damaged every day. By late August over 1.5 million children had been evacuated from [Britain's] south-east.[62]

To counter, the Allies launched a major bombing campaign to destroy V-weapon sites (Operation CROSSBOW).[63]

The V-weapons inflicted massive devastation, but the Allies adapted and responded, and from June to September 1944, "3,912 [V-1s] were brought down by anti-aircraft fire, RAF fighters and barrage balloons." Hitler had hoped these weapons would upend the British war effort but he was wrong.[64] The V-weapons did not decide the war's outcome, and, in April 1945, not long before his own death, Hitler himself acknowledged they were unsuccessful.[65]

For Eisenhower, the key point remained: His forces had landed in France, and the buildup progressed, a geographic fact that denied launch sites for the enemy's most advanced weapons.

SHOULD EISENHOWER STICK WITH ANVIL?
SHOULD HITLER FIGHT OR WITHDRAW?

On August 15, 1944, more Allied forces landed on France's southern coast. Lieutenant General Alexander "Sandy" Patch's Seventh Army, comprising troops moved from the Mediterranean Theater, landed with ease. Within one day, 66,000 Allied troops were ashore with few casualties. Hitler later called August 15 "the worst day of my life."[66] In just one month, the Allies captured key ports, took over 100,000 German prisoners, destroyed a German army, and freed southern France.[67]

Despite its success, this landing—first called ANVIL—was heavily debated by Allied leaders. (Note: The operation was later renamed DRAGOON, but for consistency we will continue to refer to it as ANVIL.) British Prime Minister Winston Churchill strongly opposed it. General Alan Brooke, Chief of the Imperial General Staff, wrote to the American Chiefs of Staff on the matter, saying: "If you insist on being damned fools, sooner than falling out with you, which would be fatal, we shall be damned fools with you."[68]

So why was there so much disagreement over a plan that worked so well? Why did Eisenhower's decision for ANVIL cause such anger among British commanders?

The Americans saw ANVIL as important for two reasons. First, it could help OVERLORD by pulling German forces from Normandy. Second, it could open a new supply route into France through Mediterranean ports. However, Churchill and the British never supported it. In the early days after the Normandy landings, the Combined Chiefs of Staff met in London from June 11 to 13, 1944. They discussed how to support OVERLORD with additional landings.[69]

Three ideas were debated: landing in southern France (ANVIL), an assault on western France to open another port, or an operation at the head of the Adriatic to push into the Balkans.[70] The decision would depend on how OVERLORD went, what the Soviets were doing, and how the Nazis responded. But no matter which option they chose, the assault would require forces and landing craft, mainly from the Mediterranean.[71]

On June 16, Eisenhower wrote to British General Henry Wilson, commander of the Mediterranean Theater:

> My belief is that we would keep more Germans away from the decisive area of northern France by landing in southern France rather than the Adriatic . . . Time is the vital factor and the overriding consideration is to launch an operation in France which holds out a reasonable prospect of success at the earliest possible date.[72]

Wilson, however, preferred an Adriatic landing that would lead to the Balkans. Eisenhower pushed back. In a June 20, 1944, message to General Marshall, Eisenhower criticized Wilson's plan:

> [Wilson] seems to discount the fact that the Combined Chiefs of Staff have long ago decided to make Western Europe the base from which to conduct decisive operations . . . To authorize any departure . . . seems to me ill advised and potentially dangerous . . . We must concentrate our forces . . . and put them into battle in the decisive theater. To do so they must all land in France and work toward a common center.[73]

A major reason for Eisenhower's urgency was the large number of American divisions waiting to fight in Britain and the United States—nearly 50 divisions total.[74] These troops needed port access to join the fight. OVERLORD's northern ports couldn't handle such scale. Opening southern ports with ANVIL was critical.

On June 23, Eisenhower wrote a long message to the Combined Chiefs of Staff. He explained why the Adriatic plan should be rejected and why ANVIL was necessary. He summarized, "OVERLORD is the decisive campaign of 1944 . . . It is imperative that we concentrate our forces in direct support of the decisive area of northern France."[75]

He concluded: "I, therefore, recommend ANVIL . . . This opens up another gateway into France . . . The possession of such a gateway I consider vital."[76]

Eisenhower emphasized that France, not the Balkans, was the decisive theater. He warned that neither Britain nor the United States had the resources to support two major European campaigns at the same time.

The US Chiefs of Staff agreed. They rejected Wilson's plan for a Balkan campaign. But the British still objected. On June 28, the British Chiefs of Staff wrote to their American counterparts asking them to reconsider. Churchill wrote directly to President Roosevelt, calling Eisenhower's position "arbitrary." He warned Roosevelt the decision would ruin "all our great affairs in the Mediterranean . . . We take it hard that this should be demanded of us." Churchill called ANVIL "bleak and sterile," and asked whether it was wise to "ruin all hopes of a major victory in Italy . . . for the sake of ANVIL with all its limitations."[77]

Roosevelt sided with Eisenhower. He wrote to Churchill: "I think we should support the views of the Supreme Allied Commander. He is definitely for ANVIL and wants action in the field by August 30th preferably earlier."[78]

The next day, June 29, Roosevelt added:

At Tehran we agreed upon a definite plan of attack . . . . Nothing has occurred to require any change . . . My dear friend, I beg you to let us go ahead with our plan.[79]

Though US leaders united behind Eisenhower, the British continued their opposition. One week before the invasion, Eisenhower wrote in his diary that the matter was still being debated:

1. The prime minister and the British chiefs of staff became interested, several days ago, in abandoning Anvil in favor of bringing additional forces into Brittany. A quick study of the proposition showed that (a) there was no assurance that we would have the Brittany ports working during the next several weeks . . .
2. Nevertheless, the British felt this was a better proposition . . .
3. I disagreed. I informed both the United States chiefs of staff and the prime minister of my flat disagreement . . .
4. This morning, August 8, a message . . . indicates that I am supported by Washington and that Anvil will go on as planned.[80]

Despite the strongest British resistance, Eisenhower's decision held. ANVIL launched as planned. It proved to be one of the most successful operations of the war. The Allies captured the ports of Marseille and Toulon and they became vital supply centers. By September 1944, these ports were supplying more troops than those in northern France.

The operation crushed a major German force and caused huge German losses. It also allowed French General Philippe Leclerc's forces to be the first Allied troops to enter Paris on August 24, 1944. Eisenhower chose Leclerc's French division (1 of 39 assigned in the campaign) to liberate the capital—giving the French people a powerful symbol of their own return.[81]

These were the results of Eisenhower's hardest-fought decision. ANVIL proved his strategic vision and his willingness to push back—even against Churchill—when he believed it was necessary.

Once the Allies established a foothold in Normandy, the invasion shifted from a beach landing to a full ground and air campaign.[82] On June 17 and again on June 29, 1944, Adolf Hitler met with his two top generals in France—Field Marshals Erwin Rommel and Gerd von Rundstedt.[83] Both told him the situation was grim and advised strategic withdrawal.

At the first meeting on June 17, Rommel provided a picture of the problem (summarized by historian Rick Atkinson):

The Allies had landed at least twenty divisions in Normandy—half a million men with 77,000 vehicles. The German Seventh Army opposed them with the equivalent of fourteen divisions, and those depleted units averaged under 11,000 men, compared with almost 17,000 a few years earlier. German casualties had reached 26,000, including more than 50 senior commanders.[84]

In just eleven days, the Allies had grown from 8 divisions (with significant casualties) on D-Day—to 20.[85] Military expert Michael O'Hanlon has explained that three things are key to a successful amphibious assault:

1. The attacker must gain air superiority.
2. The attacker must land forces where they outnumber defenders locally.
3. The attacker must build strength faster than the defender can reinforce.[86]

By June 17, the German Fifteenth Army still had 21 divisions in the Pas de Calais region—only 1 had been sent to Normandy.[87] These troops might have made a difference, but they remained in place due to the Allied deception plan known as Operation FORTITUDE. The Nazis were tricked into thinking another invasion might still come. Even weeks after D-Day, on July 3, 1944, one of Hitler's top generals told a Japanese official that General George Patton would soon land in France with 29 divisions.[88]

This failure to judge the situation correctly was damaging, but an even bigger decision lay ahead. Hitler still had a choice: Should German forces in France retreat to regroup? Or stand and fight?

His generals argued for withdrawal. Hitler refused.[89] He believed the new V-weapons would soon change the war's direction. He even suggested that those who supported falling back were cowards.[90]

In a meeting with General Alfred Jodl on July 31, Hitler said:

> We must be clear . . . Which places do we want to hold under all circumstances? We cannot throw away the harbors that keep the enemy from having unlimited manpower and material at his disposal . . . a certain number of troops are simply going to have to be sacrificed to save others.[91]

Hitler made a cold calculation.[92] He believed that by holding on to key ports, even if it cost many German lives, he could slow the Allied supply chain. That delay bought time, which he hoped would change the course of the war. Considering that each Allied soldier needed about one ton of supplies per month, Hitler's focus on ports made military sense.[93]

The strategy slowed the Allies. Cherbourg fell on June 27, 1944, but the next major ports weren't secured until September. One of those (Antwerp) wasn't fully usable until November.[94] So while Hitler's decision cost many lives, it did succeed in slowing Allied advance.

A US Army War College professor later explained this thinking: "Military commanders sell the lives of their soldiers dearly to buy things: to buy advantage, to buy opportunity, to buy victory, to buy an objective."[95]

Still, while this military logic made some sense, the impact on German leadership was severe. The tense June meetings made both Rommel and Rundstedt think they would be fired.[96] Rundstedt was removed on July 2, 1944. Rommel was badly injured in an air attack on July 17 and was later charged as a part of the July 20 plot at the Wolf's Lair in Eastern Prussia to assassinate Hitler. On October 14, 1944, other Nazi generals forced Rommel to take poison to quietly eliminate him.[97]

These leadership changes were part of a larger collapse within the Nazi high command.[98] The failed July 20, 1944, assassination plot caused Hitler to purge anyone he suspected of disloyalty:

> More than 7,000 people were arrested and 4,980 of them killed over the next few months. Sixty officers [and] twenty generals were executed . . . another thirty-six were condemned . . . fortynine committed suicide . . . At the fronts another 700 soldiers were executed.[99]

This wave of killings and suicides deeply damaged morale within the Nazi military. Even as the Nazi command structure fell apart, the Allies advanced. British forces captured Caen on July 8.[100] By late July 1944, American forces had broken through near St. Lô and were racing to Paris.[101] Commander Fritz Bayerlein, who had served under Rommel, later compared the defeat in France to the ancient Roman loss at Cannae. He wrote that no other defeat could match what happened in 1944 in terms of scale, coordination, and consequences:

[No defeat] can approach the battle of annihilation in France in 1944 in the magnitude of planning, the logic of execution, the collaboration of sea, air, and ground forces, the bulk of the booty, or the hordes of prisoners . . . its greatest strategic effect was to cement the foundation for the subsequent final and complete annihilation of the greatest military state on earth.[102]

The numbers tell the story. Between June 6 and late August 1944, Nazi casualties topped 400,000. Half were taken prisoner. In contrast, American casualties totaled 134,000, and other Allied losses were about 91,000.

Chapter 11

CONSEQUENCE: EISENHOWER AND HITLER, 1944

Humility must always be the portion of any man who receives acclaim earned in the blood of his followers and the sacrifices of his friends.
—Dwight D. Eisenhower (June 12, 1945)

n May 1944, both the Nazis and the Allies still had a chance to achieve some version of victory. The Nazis controlled France with strong forces, fortified defenses, and experienced military commanders. They had developed new weapons, like the V-1 and V-2, which Hitler judged would change the course of the war.

By the fall of 1944, the situation had changed dramatically. The Allies had captured Paris, pushed through France, and neared the German border. They had forced Hitler into the two-front war he had tried to avoid. The 1944 campaign, particularly the fighting in Normandy, became the turning point in the European Theater.[1] It had the greatest impact on how the European war ended.

Allied victories in France had major effects. The speedy Nazi retreat toward their own border showed just how effective Allied leadership had been. As one report put it, this "yielded unmistakable evidence of massive positive strategic effect achieved by Allied command performance."[2]

Several key gains came from this campaign. First, before the invasion, the Allies had no base on the European mainland from which to launch a direct attack on Nazi Germany. The success at Normandy gave them a strong foothold from which they could move inland. Without this, defeating the Nazis on land would have been nearly impossible.

Second, the Soviets needed help. Since 1942, Soviet leader Joseph Stalin had asked the Allies to open a second front. While the Soviets had made progress in the East, the cost in lives was enormous. A new front in the West would provide the Soviets much-needed relief.

Third, the Allied advance through France ultimately denied Nazi use of the V-weapons. These weapons damaged British morale, and Hitler hoped they would force the British to surrender.[3] By capturing French territory, the Allies ended Germany's ability to launch them at will.

Other practical advantages followed. The German navy lost key Atlantic ports. The Allies also cut off land routes to Spain and Portugal. This blocked German access to important raw materials that had been smuggled from the Iberian Peninsula.

In short, by taking France, the Allies denied Hitler his terror weapons, opened a second front to help the Soviets, gained control of vital ports, and isolated Germany from important supplies. The Nazis, meanwhile, were now facing invasion from both East and West and had no good way to strike back. Without these Allied victories made possible by Eisenhower's superior decisions, the war's outcome might have been very different. Eisenhower changed the game.

As well as the campaign's consequences went for the Allies, so too can we learn a great deal from Eisenhower's strategic leadership—particularly, some of the traits he demonstrated.

Like humility. One of Eisenhower's early biographers was struck by how Eisenhower never saw power as belonging to him personally (in contrast with Hitler). Instead, he treated it as something he was responsible for—but not entitled to.[4] Some have questioned the sincerity of Eisenhower's humility.[5] But two moments from 1944 and 1945 suggest it was real, very real.

The first example is the scribbled note he drafted before D-Day in case the invasion failed. In his own handwriting, Eisenhower edited a passive sentence—"the troops have been withdrawn"—into the active "I have withdrawn the troops." He deliberately inserted personal agency in a way that demonstrated his willingness to shoulder blame.[6]

The second is his final message after Germany's surrender. His staff had drafted several grand, elegant, victorious statements. Eisenhower rejected them all. He instead wrote: "The mission of this Allied force was fulfilled at 0241 local time, May 7th, 1945."[7]

That quiet line summed up Eisenhower's leadership—focused not on glory but on duty. On results. After all the tough calls and heavy responsibilities, Eisenhower met success with humility and potential failure with personal accountability. Rare traits in any strategic leader, and especially in one who helped win the most destructive war in history.

Shortly after the war, Eisenhower gave a speech at London's Guildhall, which he wrote himself at night after long workdays over the months following the Nazi surrender. He revised it carefully and delivered the line that would later be etched on his tombstone: "Humility must always be the portion of any man who receives acclaim earned in the blood of his followers and the sacrifices of his friends." The British press warmly welcomed the speech, comparing it to the Gettysburg Address. Eisenhower called that review an "excess of friendly misjudgment."[8]

Our modern strategic leaders, our gray beards, affirmed Eisenhower's approach just in the way they each conducted themselves. Despite the fact that society seems to be trending in the other direction, all were humble. It was self-evident in their every syllable. As General Neller put it, "Humility's in short supply these days." Neller specified that he never thought he would rise to be the Marine Corps commandant because, bluntly, his "name was never on that list." So he never had any "intention of doing that job." For Neller it was always important to remember, "Never think you're better than everybody else," because "the force needs to know that you share the risk and the families need to know you care about them."

Why? Because when you're spending human lives—part of a system that orders some into extreme risk—it matters that you actually believe the lives you're spending are as important as your own. People won't carry out those awful but necessary orders unless they believe in the person that's making the order.

"How," asked Rear Admiral Studeman, "do you tap into the deepest motivations?" By spending great amounts of time on the "human elements," forging personal connections bit by bit, "little light touches" that are almost like "constant gardening."

Lieutenant General Chris Miller pointed out that we should seek a person for strategic leadership "who contains some contradictions," an individual with "true intellectual humility." That seems a little like a tall order. Consider, however, that we know "the idea that a person can know everything is just completely ridiculous. But knowing who to trust, when to ask the right questions, when to take information on board and how much of it to take on board. You have to be truly intellectually open and humble."

What does all this add up to? Humility always, but imbued with an underlying persistent confidence to cut down inferior ideas in service of some important objective. One modern professional football player has called this special combination "humble confidence."[9]

How can we create that seemingly contradictory combination? Mentorship—following a personal, human, good example—was the pathway for many strategic leaders.

It turns out it's easier to climb if someone shows you the way. All five gray beards gushed with appreciation for those that helped them find their footing at some stage of their career. General Austin Miller, given a choice between historical figures and personal mentors, launched in by saying, "Let me talk about real-life people first." What stood out from conversation with the gray beards were the decades-long relationships with several mentors, which included Major General Bill Garrison, General Stan McChrystal ("I thought he was maybe the most brilliant guy I had met"), and General Joe Dunford ("still my mentor today"), to name just a few.

General Neller had a similar relationship with General Dunford, calling him "maybe the best Marine I ever met in my life."* Rear Admiral Studeman's father was himself a four-star flag officer and served as the director of the National Security Agency. Through his father, Studeman met many "intelligent, decent, strong-willed, iron-minded people [each] with a transcendent cause."

But for most it was less about rank than personal lessons. General Neller had a tactics instructor who earned "a battlefield commission from Vietnam after 18 years as a Marine. He grew up in eastern North Carolina, did not own a pair of shoes until he joined the Marine Corps." The instructor was "really hard and cold, but then as I got to know him, as I

---

* Four of five gray beards explicitly mentioned General Joe Dunford, former chairman of the Joint Chiefs, making him a military version of "Six Degrees of Kevin Bacon." Dunford obviously had a large and wide impact on the military while he served in senior leadership.

worked for him, he was really kind, generous, tough but fair guy. And he was really smart about people." He taught Neller "the way we do stuff" so well that nearly 50 years later, the lessons are still present.

For Lieutenant General Chris Miller, same thing. When he was mid-career, another officer, slightly more senior, taught him how to lead an air crew and create a tight team. "I was his copilot and what he showed me in the time we were on a crew together, which is about ten months, was how to be an air crew commander. In short, he made it clear we'd discuss and decide actions as a crew when time allowed, and he'd make decisions alone if time was short—but either way, he took responsibility. The value of teamwork and accountability were both crystal clear." General Breedlove reported being shaped by "four or five great leaders" in his career, and told one story that'd stuck with him for decades. One particular officer he worked under pointedly "would not use the military phone to call his wife" from an assignment in Germany, and instead would "walk down the hall and put coins in the pay phone" to call her. It's this constant stream of watching the right way to do things, sometimes completely unintentional. The other, more direct version Breedlove calls the American military's "intense desire" to train those coming up behind. He described it almost as an invisible ladder where those above constantly look for ways to lend a hand up to those ascending from below. West Point calls this the "Long Gray Line."

It was the same for Eisenhower.

After graduating from West Point, Eisenhower had a series of formative experiences. In 1919, he participated in a cross-country motor convoy meant to test US mobilization capability. Later, he worked with then–Colonel George S. Patton. They "got along famously" and developed a "comprehensive tank doctrine" with the "enthusiasm of zealots."[10]

In 1922, after the death of his infant son, Eisenhower was sent to Panama, where he met Brigadier General Fox Conner—one of the most important mentors in his life. Conner sparked Eisenhower's interest in the military profession and steered him toward serious self-education.

Eisenhower later explained that he had grown to dislike military history because at West Point, it had been taught as pure memorization. He recalled: "Little attempt was made to explain the meaning of the battle, why it came about, what the commanders hoped to accomplish . . . If this was military history, I wanted no part of it."[11]

Conner didn't argue. Instead, he invited Eisenhower to his quarters, showed him his library, and lent him historical novels like *The Long Roll* and *The Exploits of Brigadier Gerard*. Conner asked, "Wouldn't you like to know something of what the armies were actually doing during the period of the novels you've just read?" That sparked Eisenhower's interest. Conner then had him read military history—Grant's and Sheridan's memoirs, Clausewitz's *On War* (three times), and works on the Civil War, like Steele's *Campaigns*. Eisenhower wrote, "As I began to absorb the material . . . we spent many hours in analyzing its campaigns."[12]

This guided reading, combined with serious conversation, must have helped Eisenhower develop strategic thinking and judgment. It also set him on a course that helped him graduate first in his class at the Army Command and General Staff School in 1926—a key mid-career achievement.

In 1928, Eisenhower, with his wife's encouragement, accepted a second tour in France with the American Battle Monuments Commission. This gave him a better understanding of French military history, geography, and culture—skills that would later prove useful during the Allied campaign in France.[13] In experiencing the environment he would someday fight over, Eisenhower probably prepared better for World War II than in any other way.

In 1936, Eisenhower was sent to the Philippines with Major General Douglas MacArthur. While there, Eisenhower developed broad geopolitical thinking. He earned a pilot's license and gained over 350 hours of flying experience, which helped him later to better understand airpower. He also advised the Philippine president on topics beyond defense, including "taxes, education, [and] honesty in government."[14]

Eisenhower's performance benefited greatly from these wide and varied experiences. With such remarkable opportunities for individual improvement, he must have built a truly independent mind. Balanced, too, with the ability to take in new ideas and situations, and, even in the worst, highest-pressure situations, to make clear and effective and superior decisions.

Dwight Eisenhower commanded some of the largest formations ever and won a lasting victory in Europe. Perhaps the best compliment he earned the hardest way from one of his toughest critics. Prime Minister Winston Churchill wrote to Eisenhower just before the invasion,

If by Christmas you have succeeded in liberating our beloved Paris, if she can by [that] time regain her life of freedom and take her accustomed place as a center of Western European culture and beauty, then I will proclaim that this operation is the most grandly conceived and best conducted known to the history of warfare.

Eisenhower, in reply, simply recorded his (accurate) prediction: "Mr. Prime Minister, we expect to be on the borders of Germany by Christmas, pounding away at her defenses."[15]

He called it. And in so doing, earned Churchill's praise for the "most grandly conceived and best conducted" operation "known to the history of warfare."

Part V

THE ART OF THE BETTER DECISION

Chapter 12

WHO WINS WARS

If the mind is to emerge unscathed from this relentless struggle with the unforeseen, two qualities are indispensable: first, an intellect that, even in the darkest hour, retains some glimmerings of the inner light which leads to truth; and second, the courage to follow this faint light wherever it may lead. The first of these qualities is described by the French term, coup d'oeil; *the second is determination.*
—Carl von Clausewitz

The aim of all strategic leadership is the application of superior judgment.

Now it's on us to figure out a way—based on the breadcrumbs Washington, Grant, and Eisenhower left for us in moments of true American peril—to access the art of the better decision. Of course, this is an art, not a science, because we know every future challenge will have its own unique aspects.

We've seen better judgment in action, so now let's look under the hood to what potentially powered those performances. Because if we want to change the game like they did, then we ought to study where they came from.

What inputs led to such extraordinary outputs?

While each strategic leader was different, their character and style contain some common threads.

Washington and Eisenhower were about six feet tall; Grant was around five feet, eight inches tall.[1] Their personalities differed: Eisenhower was cheerful and positive, Grant was mostly stoic and serious, and Washington could be steady in public but gloomy in private letters.[2] Grant was a cigar smoker, and Eisenhower smoked four packs of cigarettes a day, but there's no record of Washington using tobacco during the war (despite having grown it at Mount Vernon).[3]

From a modern perspective, they were relatively young supreme commanders. British military theorist and major general J. F. C. Fuller took seriously the impact of age on generalship. In an appendix to his book, *Generalship*, he listed the ages of one hundred well-known and well-regarded historical generals up to the year 1866 (a date after which he believed "generalship becomes senile"). Fuller noted the average age on his list was just over 40 years old, and that 74% were 45 or younger. From this, Fuller theorized that the "period of most efficient generalship lies between the years thirty and forty-nine," with peak performance occurring "between the years thirty-five and forty-five" (for his part, Grant said he would never "put a general in the field over fifty").[4] On balance, Fuller believed that youth in generalship was an asset and an advantage. This idea has support in other areas—like a study by the US National Bureau of Economic Research showing most Nobel Prize winners developed their important ideas between ages 35 and 39.[5]

The cases mostly align with this theory of relative youth. Washington was 44 in 1776; Grant was 42 in 1864; Eisenhower was 53 in 1944.

Their opponents were older: Howe was 47, Lee was 57, and Hitler was 54. While Eisenhower was slightly above Fuller's range, the trend shows youth may offer an advantage in strategic leadership.

All three supreme commanders also sat on top of potentially volcanic tempers, which by accounts never impacted their decision-making ability, and they were mostly able to hold these in check while at war.[6] They learned to hold their tempers in even after the battlefield and back in civilian life.

FROM WAR TO PEACE: THEIR PRESIDENCIES

All three commanders later became two-term American presidents. This suggests two things. First, it shows that successful generals often possess some political skill. Second, it hints that leadership in war can carry over into peace.

None were political partisans while in uniform. They deferred to their civilian leaders and avoided any political ambition during the war.[7] That probably helped build trust with elected leaders and allowed them to rise later.

As presidents, all three protected what they had won in war. Washington's job was to unite a loose collection of states into one country. His war ended colonial rule; his presidency built a new nation.[8] Grant preserved the Union at war and then protected freedmen's rights during Reconstruction.[9] Eisenhower, after defeating Nazi Germany, shaped a relatively peaceful world order during a tense phase of the Cold War. As one historian put it, Eisenhower "safely guided the free world through one of the most dangerous decades."[10]

George Washington was famously called "first in war, first in peace."

That same line applies to Grant and Eisenhower. They won wars as generals, then held on to peace as presidents. While not every wartime commander needs to become president, their political leadership helped make sure the victories on the battlefield translated into lasting change.

The theorist Carl von Clausewitz described war in two ways. He said war is "an act of force to compel our enemy to do our will." Also, war is "a continuation of political intercourse."[11] This way of thinking sees two sides of war, which the scholar Gideon Rose has written about: one "negative," "coercive," and mostly about combat; the other "positive" and "constructive," centering on "politics."[12] Those that look upon war in a similarly comprehensive way are likely to see that Washington, Grant, and Eisenhower may have been successful, in part, because they fulfilled both halves of Clausewitz's theoretical vision of war, first as military leaders and then as political leaders.

THE POWER OF WORDS

All three men were skilled writers and communicators. Their letters, orders, and speeches were often composed under pressure, but were still clear, calm, and persuasive.

A classicist once said that Julius Caesar was rare because he was "a great general, a great politician, and also a great author."[13] But maybe Caesar wasn't so rare—that same praise could apply equally to Washington, Grant, and Eisenhower.

Washington wrote thousands of letters that still impress readers today.[14] His style was steady and thoughtful, even when writing in crisis. Grant's memoirs are considered one of the best works of military literature ever written.[15] Eisenhower's documents from World War II are full of direct, strong language. After the war, he wrote several books and gave famous speeches, including the Guildhall Address in London. Not all writers are superior strategic leaders, but these superior strategic leaders were all writers.

LEARNING AND EXPERIENCE

In variable amounts, all three showed an indifference for official education, or even didn't attend formal schooling. Yet all displayed a passion for self-study, and all had some meaningful military experience prior to the wars in which they served as strategic leaders. Washington had little in the way of an education, but his desire to learn is on display with one quick look at his personal library, with subjects ranging from veterinary care to books on poetry, to religion, philosophy, geography, and law. Importantly, he had a clear interest in military subjects, particularly his British adversaries.[16]

Grant didn't love West Point, but he liked math and later became an avid reader.[17] After university, Grant's superlative reading went a step further as he demonstrated the ability to put himself into the place and mind of other military commanders.[18] He also had combat experience in the Mexican War. Eisenhower wasn't a top student at West Point, either, but he gained leadership skills through sports and teamwork.[19] His real education came later, especially through mentorship under Brigadier General Fox Conner and experiences in Washington, Panama, and the Philippines. He learned doctrine, strategy, and how to manage large teams.

None of them followed any sort of perfect path. But each man took responsibility for his own growth. They combined book knowledge with experience. They asked questions, learned from others, and used those lessons in wartime.

EARLY HARDSHIP AND CHILDHOOD RESILIENCE

All three faced significant setbacks in younger years. George Washington's early life was the most tragic, having sustained the death of his father at age 11, and then, at age 20, the loss of his half-brother Lawrence, who had become a "surrogate father." Washington also always felt educationally deficient, having only finished grade school.[20] Grant had a domineering father who attempted to manipulate and live through his son, so much so that, without telling Ulysses, his father essentially pushed him single-handedly into West Point.[21] Eisenhower's family was poor in his early years, the result of a father who was repeatedly swindled and suffered business disaster.[22]

These childhood struggles seem to reflect a larger trend. In 1962, two researchers studied the backgrounds of hundreds of successful people and found that most of them had experienced some sort of adversity in their youth. The study noted that these individuals often came from homes where learning and intellectual curiosity were valued. They frequently disliked formal schooling but loved learning on their own. Most had at least one strong, supportive parent—usually a mother—who believed in them.[23]

More than 90% came from families that encouraged learning and had a strong drive toward achievement. Over 75% had difficult childhoods caused by poverty, broken homes, overly controlling parents, physical or mental challenges, or failure in school. The study concluded that facing hardship early in life helped many of these people develop the resilience needed for later success.[24] These findings would seem to affirm that a challenge in childhood builds resiliency in high-performing individuals.[25]

The early lives of Washington, Grant, and Eisenhower fit this pattern. Winston Churchill once noted, "Solitary trees, if they grow at all, grow strong: and a boy deprived of a father's care often develops . . . an independence and a vigor of thought."[26] Another well-known but more modern (and wealthy) business figure, Larry Ellison, once said, "I had all the disadvantages necessary for success."[27]

For Washington, Grant, and Eisenhower, difficulty in youth may have helped build the strength they later used in strategic leadership.

Does all this mean we have to be well-spoken presidents who've overcome childhood obstacles to defeat our older adversaries?

Even if those experiences might strengthen us—no. The reality is that these types of observable characteristics only take us so far. What truly separates us is how we think. And while we can't peer directly into the thoughts and minds of these historical strategic leaders, we can make inferences to better understand what was going on in their minds in order to build up our own strategic leader's mindset.

SHADOW BOXING AND CULTIVATING AN INDIFFERENCE TO OUTCOME

In July 1861, the Civil War had only just begun. Ulysses S. Grant was a newly promoted colonel, given command of a regiment and following a Confederate force led by a Colonel Thomas Harris (someone Grant knew from West Point). Grant wrote:

As we approached the brow of the hill from which it was expected we could see [the Confederates'] camp, and possible find his men ready formed to meet us, my heart kept getting higher and higher until it felt to me as though it was in my throat. I would have given anything then to have been back in Illinois, but I had not the moral courage to halt and consider what to do; I kept right on. When we reached a point from which the valley below was in full view I halted. The place where [the Confederates] had been encamped a few days before was still there and the marks of a recent encampment were plainly visible, but the troops were gone. My heart resumed its place. It occurred to me at once that Harris [the Confederate commander] had been as much afraid of me as I had been of him. This was a view of the question I had never taken before; but it was one I never forgot afterwards. From that event to the close of the war, I never experienced trepidation upon confronting an enemy, though I always felt more or less anxiety. I never forgot that he had as much reason to fear my forces as I had his. The lesson was valuable.[28]

Grant's lesson points to two takeaways.

The first is the value of shadow boxing. Almost a century later, in 1957, at the height of the Cold War, Herman Kahn cowrote a paper for RAND on strategic planning for an uncertain world.[29] Kahn wrote about the "Informal Game" strategists ought to play while thinking through threats. "This is a conscious attempt to try to take account of the enemy's reactions. It is sometimes played inside one man's head. One simply asks himself," wrote Kahn, "what would the enemy do if I did this," or "what does he think I will do if he does such and such?"

Kahn called it "Informal," but it's more like mental shadow boxing. Prize fighters need sparring partners and shadow-work just as strategic leaders need thought experiments and hypothetical adversaries.

That's where shadow boxing comes in. It's not a full war game. It's not a full critical analysis. It is an informal, individual, imaginative strategic study of the adversary and the conflict.

Shadow boxing has three principal virtues. First, it is free, completely free of cost. You need only your own mind to play. Second, because it is a mental exercise, it is recoverable. Nobody need die. And third, depending on the exercise's degree and depth, this is meaningful practice. You can think through your thrusts and the opponent's parries, you can anticipate adversary advances and your defenses, you can pre-experience the course of the conflict, all in your own mind.

What might it look like in real life?

Shadow boxing works in all walks of life. Business, government, non-profits, sports, and even in one's own personal life.

Grant's second takeaway for us is to cultivate calm in competition. To value a certain indifference to outcome. There's a moment on screen that captured this when the actor Richard Gere played a knight teaching another his approach to sword fighting.

> *KNIGHT: You have to know that one moment in every fight when you*
> *win or lose and you have to know to wait for it.*
> *STUDENT: I can do that.*
> *KNIGHT: And you have to not care whether you live or die.*

Indifference to outcome. For some that might seem a mistake. Shouldn't we care, deeply care, about whether we win or lose, succeed or fail? Isn't that all that matters? Heck, isn't that what Green Bay Packers coach (and legend) Vince Lombardi said: "Winning isn't everything, it's the only thing." The *only* thing.

Let's acknowledge some nuance here. Yes, outcome matters. We want to succeed at what we're doing. The world exists in some way and we want to succeed in changing it according to our desires, whether that be defeating an adversary, earning a contract over competitors, or winning a championship over rivals. So yes, outcome matters.

But just the same, it matters that we can approach these competitions and challenges with indifference in our hearts and minds. No matter the outcome of any given trial—except for exactly once in our lives, when we meet our end—we will have to get up and go for another round tomorrow. So it behooves the strategic leader to cultivate a sense of indifference to the outcome of any given challenge.

Of course, sword fighting in movies isn't strategic leadership. But we can see Grant's approach echoes what was on screen. We'd do well to seek the same.

EMBRACE THE "I" IN STRATEGY (OR, WHEN IN CHARGE, TAKE CHARGE)

Two moments from Eisenhower's earlier command days—prior to 1944—provide some insight into his mentality in strategic leadership.

In 1942, Eisenhower had to make a quick decision about the surrender of a particular Vichy French admiral who still had forces serving under him. Eisenhower knew there would be political blowback among the Allies (especially the British). Here is how he recorded the encounter and decision at the time:

The military advantages of an immediate cease fire are so overwhelming [that we must take the offer, but] . . . none of this should be under any misapprehensions as to what the consequences of this action may be. In both our nations, [Vichy French Admiral] Darlan is a deep-dyed villain. When public opinion raises its outcry our two governments will be embarrassed. Because of this, we'll act so quickly that reports to our governments will be on the basis of action *taken* . . . If public opinion becomes too inflamed because we seem guilty of dealing with the enemy, the governments must be free to disavow us and indeed remove us from our posts.[30]

In anticipating and navigating the consequences, Eisenhower revealed his willingness to be held accountable for his own strategic decisions—a quality that earned him trust with his political superiors. When in charge, he took charge.

Another story about Pantelleria, a minuscule island in the Mediterranean, is just as instructive. In Eisenhower's words:

Halfway between the northern tip of Tunisia and the island of Sicily, Pantelleria was heavily garrisoned by Italians. Popularly, it was said to be the "Gibraltar of the Central Mediterranean." The coastline was rocky, with no beaches, and the only approach was by sea through a narrow harbor perhaps three hundred yards wide. The interior was hilly, cut up into small plots by stone walls. Its capture would be a difficult feat of arms if the place were garrisoned by good, sturdy troops. It was almost out of question to attack by airborne method; descending soldiers, blown up against the stone walls by prevailing winds, would be almost 100 percent casualties. In the circumstances, some thought that the island was unassailable and that it would be foolish to try to take it.

There were other elements to consider, I thought. One was the fact that with the landing strip on the top of the island in possession of the enemy, our convoys going across from Africa to Sicily would be subject to strafing and dive-bomber attack. We would be denied the use of the field for both defense and offensive operations. My belief was that the officers and men of the Italian Army were sick of the war and wanted to get out of it. We knew that Mussolini had given orders that if any of the Italian garrisons surrendered, their families at home would pay the penalty. But with the theory that morale is the telling factor in war and suspecting that Italian morale was at a low ebb, I insisted on attempting the island's capture.

While Eisenhower's personal staff agreed with him, strong opposition came from British ground commanders who were concerned about risking "failure." In the end, when the attack on the little island commenced, "the men in the landing ships had not even completed getting into their landing craft when white flags began to appear all over the island."[31] Eisenhower's gut call was correct.

All strategy, and strategic leadership, begins with an "I." Strategy formulation's first step is, and always will be, the individual idea. There is no instance in all of recorded history for the exact same idea to occur in every mind at the exact same moment. It's just not possible.[32]

Strategy starts with the recognition that something needs to change and—bang!—here's an idea for change. That requires an individual to step forward with an idea. That individual must first formulate the idea, even at a crude level, even at a level others would disagree with, at a level that may not even make full sense at first whack.

Of course, strategy is also a team sport. Anything worth doing with an eye to strategy will be done as a team effort. But at inception, strategy and strategic decision begin in a single mind.

That's why, if you squint, there's an "I" in strategy. It's silent. Almost impossible to hear. Nearly imperceptible.

Every scenario the strategic leader faces demands a new approach. Imagine a sports team that plays the same opponent on consecutive nights. While the coach's strategy may be similar both nights, it won't be the exact same because the second match will be influenced—and changed—by the first.

Be like Eisenhower. When in charge, take charge, and always remember the "I" in strategy and use it for motivation to come up with new ideas for new challenges.

SUCCESS REQUIRES OPTIMISM

Successful strategic leaders must always travel a dark road of despair to get to the dawn that brings gains. Optimism is required on this difficult path, which is a large part of what has made America's top supreme commanders effective and victorious.[33]

With far fewer men and military assets, and having been beaten by the British in battle after battle across New York, Washington was forced to withdraw to New Jersey. So bleak was the moment that Thomas Paine wrote that "these are the times that try men's souls." And we've covered that, privately, Washington succumbed to pessimism, admitted in personal dispatches that the Continentals might lose, and told his estate manager that December 1776 to "have my Papers" ready to move if the British were to win and send forces to (likely destroy) Washington's home.[34]

Yet, dire as the situation was, Washington never gave up. Had he wavered or succumbed to defeatism, Americans would all be taking a keener interest in cricket. Instead, Washington roused his men, asked them to be "resolve[d] to conquer or die" and to "animate and encourage each other" through the tough times on the rough road to a long and hard-fought victory.

Or consider Lieutenant General Ulysses Grant in 1864. He was far from the first of Lincoln's commanders, but unlike his predecessors, he knew well the human cost to be paid to win out over Lee's Confederate army. Grant did not waver in his core conviction that the Confederates were on their "last man," as he wrote to Elihu Washburne on August 16, 1864.[35] He kept hammering away until Lee was backed into Richmond's ramparts, ultimately to surrender.

General Dwight Eisenhower's experience in 1944 is another useful data point on the power of optimism in arduous command circumstances. Adolf Hitler had made the French coast a Nazi priority, and even sent one of his most talented commanders, Field Marshal Erwin Rommel, to sharpen the defenses there. The job of rolling back Rommel's fortifications fell to Eisenhower. In private, Eisenhower felt the weight of the invasion's key decisions, and he wrote that it would be "difficult to conceive of a more soul-racking problem." He famously authored two separate public statements about the invasion's outcome—one to use if it worked, and one if the operation failed.

We of course know what happened. The paratroopers succeeded at softening up the Nazi defenses for the Allied amphibious landings. The

Allies went on to take Paris, liberate the rest of France, and defeat the Nazis.

So what should we take from this brief survey of successful strategic leadership?

None of these strategic leaders were infallible. At times, Washington, Grant, and Eisenhower questioned themselves and their judgments. But then, who wouldn't in such terrible circumstances, duty bound to spend certain young lives and national wealth at war in pursuit of uncertain strategic gains and political decisions? And so, yes, they did despair and could be privately negative.

Yet, in such circumstances, outward optimism is a general's greatest asset. Hope must be in the strategic leader's DNA—without it, the whole enterprise would rot from the top down.

George Orwell once rightly pointed out that the fastest way to end a war is to lose it. But surely a corollary must be that the mind of the strategic leader is the first place wars are lost. No cancer kills more quickly than a leader lacking public faith in the endeavor.

America is far better off with generals imbued with the right touch of indefatigable optimism. Because without this trait, America would be doomed to defeat after defeat—indeed, the country likely wouldn't even exist.

Chapter 13

HOW WE CHANGE THE GAME

There are some very real minds that "will, sooner or later,
as they have in the past, have a profound effect on our
nation and on our society and its civilization."
—J. C. Wylie

Let's return to our initial ambition—to study who wins wars, and learn what we can from those who do. Now's the part of the story when we pocket those lessons for our own use—so that we can change our own game.

Wouldn't it be so much easier if we could just pull on one of Napoleon's famous black hats and step into his mind? In 2018, the one he wore for his defeat at the Battle of Waterloo sold at auction for $400,000.[1] What would it be like to think like him? To know his thoughts after so many years of wars, victories, and losses? Even to know his mistakes would be valuable, far more than a few hundred grand.

Once upon a time we looked in some strange places for insight into human greatness. Like Albert Einstein's brain—literally.

When Albert Einstein passed away on April 18, 1955, Princeton Hospital's Dr. Thomas Harvey conducted an autopsy. Once the autopsy was complete, Harvey removed Einstein's brain and kept it for himself. Strange as it sounds, as "the legal status of corpses is complicated," so Harvey was not prosecuted for what might otherwise seem a ridiculous crime.[2]

Upon hearing of the theft of Einstein's brain, Lieutenant Colonel (and medical doctor) Webb Haymaker of the US Armed Forces Institute of Pathology "summoned Harvey to Washington, in full knowledge that the Soviets were studying their own elite brains."[3] Ten years earlier, while with the same military organization, Haymaker examined the brain of Benito Mussolini after American soldiers recovered it in 1945. Despite several requests, Haymaker couldn't get Harvey to let him study Einstein's brain.[4]

But even if Haymaker had gotten his chance, this attempt would have failed then too. There is no surefire identifiable marker for genius, just as there isn't one for superior strategic leadership. We can't just peek at some brain tissue or genetic code to figure out who'll be a successful strategic leader.

How could we? Especially when the variables of some far-off contest are as yet unknown, the field of play and adversary yet to be selected.

On some level we're seeking something impossible. For the military, it's to prepare someone for a unique wartime environment with the highest stakes. That's an almost unreachable bar. Imagine Washington, imagine Grant, imagine Eisenhower, imagine all of them stepping into their moment. Not just them, but others at similarly dizzying heights at similarly disorienting moments. Perhaps successful strategic leadership always feels like an impossible task.

How do we pick the right person for the job?

Some might simply lean into a Darwinian approach. It feels like such an elegant answer. *Let's just fire our way to success.*

There's a long history of firing generals. When the Spartan Brasidas took Thucydides by surprise at Amphipolis, the Athenians "held Thucydides responsible for its defeat and convicted him of treason, sending him off to exile for the twenty years that remained" in the Peloponnesian War.[5] Or consider John Adams, effectively the American secretary of war during the Revolutionary War, who wrote to his wife Abigail in mid-August 1777: "I think we shall never defend a Post, until we shoot a general. After that we shall defend posts . . . We must trifle no more."[6] So there is a historical lineage to strict accountability measures for generals.

But there are several problems here. The first is that we may not have the time to waste on inferior strategic leaders on the road to the one we need. A Darwinian approach also neglects the fact that many, if not all, strategic leaders grow into their challenges. Many commanders over time—including Washington, Grant, and Eisenhower—suffered tactical setbacks early in their careers only to grow to become truly superior, war-winning strategic leaders.

There are also strategic leaders who fit in certain environments ("horses for courses," as the adage goes). Fit applies to an adversary too; the adversary often does more to shape the strategic leader than any other individual.[7]

Of course, accountability is a necessary part of building, selecting, and wielding military leaders, just as it is in many fields of elite leadership. But it will never be sufficient for finding the superior strategic leaders we need.

Another, more modern instinct might be to simply rely on artificial intelligence (AI). Turn strategic leadership over to the machines. Load them up with all the strategic writing, all the strategic information, and just "StratChatGPT" our way through our next war or national crisis.

But the higher the stakes, the more people's lives are impacted, the less deferential humanity will be to machine-made decisions. Strategic leadership must always come with a heartbeat and fingertip feel. Think back to the nuanced complexity of the trade-off Washington negotiated in 1776, the personal pain Grant's 1864 campaign inflicted, the sadness and fear Eisenhower felt in spending so many young lives in 1944. An inherent humanity was inextricably part of their superior performance in strategic leadership. When you spend human lives and effort, when you do anything of significance to alter human affairs—that requires a human brain and body. It may help at the margins, but AI will never replace strategic leadership. Ever.

How do you prepare someone—anyone—for supreme command in a war for the very highest stakes? How do you prepare someone to succeed as Washington, as Grant, as Eisenhower—with so much hanging in the balance? How do you educate and grow this person?

You can't. Well—*we* can't.

When I consulted our gray-beard brain trust for their modern take on what it takes, there was some strong agreement. Informal self-study matters far more than formal education in building success. Think podcast listening, newspaper reading, and essay writing—over degrees attained and diplomas achieved. That doesn't mean we throw away military schools. But a successful supreme commander a War College alone cannot make.

General Austin Miller was once told he was "destroying" his career as a young officer when he took a six-month assignment that put him alongside Salvadoran cadets and officers at war. This led him to a "richness of experiences" that helped him "grow into" strategic leadership over time. General Neller affirmed the same, that the "position you end up in drives your thought process" to such a degree that growth comes naturally. Rear Admiral Studeman recalled walking down a hallway filled with pictures and biographies of senior naval officers. Over time he read the biographies more closely and noticed "none of them were the same." The "diversity of experience" is what stood out most. Studeman broke out of the "straitjacket of careerism" to take risks to get to that next great learning experience that will make a person "more capable as a strategic leader."

General Breedlove described learning a lot from another senior officer who advised, "You've got to paint the white lines on the road, and if your people get outside the white lines, you need to smack them in the head and get them back inside the white lines. But do not grab the wheel. Let them drive." This kind of latitude takes trust, but also must encourage the development of strategic leadership skills over time.

Lieutenant General Chris Miller had an early, memorable assignment working with the secretary of the Air Force. He traveled to Israel and Egypt. He listened in on a conversation with the vice president. He saw the secretary (appropriately) rip into a four-star general. His gut sense was that great strategic leaders benefit from getting these remarkable windows into experience, and down the road they "self-identify," reveal themselves.

It seems there is no step-by-step roadmap that guides someone to be a superior strategic leader. But we don't necessarily need one. We don't need a "secret weapon," as Lieutenant General Miller put it, but we can create a "variety" of experiences that ensures we find someone better than anyone on the other side of the field. All roads lead to the mountaintop—you've just got to be smart enough, strong enough, and brave enough to make the climb.

Maybe you're reading this because you want to be a strategic leader. Maybe you're reading because you're in the military and you hope to ascend to supreme command. Maybe you're reading as a human resources professional and want some bread crumbs that might lead you to your next best hire. Maybe you're into history and learning how great generals got so great. Maybe you're a CEO or a coach and you want a little edge. And maybe you're a citizen, charged with selecting the best strategic leaders to take us into tomorrow.

By now you know that superior decision-making is the difference in strategic leadership. You know that it can be seen in a cycle, in contrast with an adversary, and only fully evaluated in hindsight. You know that there are some common characteristics that seem to attend this superior performance, including empathy, grit, and humility.

And you know that a strategic leader's role looks a lot like a funnel. A range of ideas and options goes in the top and only one choice, formed into a powerful force, emerges from the bottom. Yet it seems that funnel's shape is changing in two big ways.

It's growing wider at the top as more options and tools become available to the strategic leader. And the water is flowing faster through the funnel, in that communication and minds are moved more quickly than ever by events.

Even so, strategic leaders to come will still close with and destroy their adversaries with the art of the better decision.

But this funnel is just a metaphor. In our real world the funnel represents people, actual people, and those people are also changing with the times. And so strategic leadership will look a little different in a few ways.

Strategic leadership is on the way to generational turnover that applies equally to those in uniform and beyond.

In 2030, the Greatest Generation will be gone. The baby boomers will be retired.

Generation X will be the generals and strategic leaders; millennials will be mid-career field grades, and Generation Z (and Alpha) will be developing as cadets and company commanders. But there's a flashing red light there—the Cold War and what came before will be dead to our entire senior military leadership. They will have no experience with earthquakes of extreme violence or truly global, great power wars (even the cold kind).

If the American military's professional sin of the past generation was forgetting counterinsurgency, then big war amnesia looms large in coming years as the sin of the next. As with all generational shifts, future leaders will be prisoners of the problems of their day, but also blind to some of the problems of the past. This same issue plagues nonmilitary organizations too. That's why disciplined study of the past—and mentorship—matter so much to create context for newly emerging scenarios and how they relate to past problems.

How else might the strategic leadership funnel change in coming years?

The funnel will get more global. All major American allies are in demographic decline. It's one thing to not want to spend blood or treasure, it's another thing entirely to not have enough young people or defense dollars to spend. This will mean more multinational operations, overseas assignments, and international engagement. Business, sport, education—indeed, all facets of life have expanded geographically with technology and travel.

Strategic leaders will need to become more technical. As threats expand with technological advancement, so too will the need to possess requisite technical and scientific literacy. Think of the criticality of information that flows online. Every strategic leader must account for this factor.

They must also be more narrative focused. Traditionally, strategic leaders focus on some blend of fighting and policy. But there's a third arena that's taken off in the information age: narrative. Getting the other side to believe in and observe your story matters more than it used to now that everyone has access to unlimited information. *The better story wins* seems like an adage with endless applicability.

Strategic leadership's look and feel will change. Senior military command will be more meritocratic. Public belief in the gray-haired, experienced WASP male at the head of an institution has been shaken; the American people have grown more comfortable with young (and different) leaders in positions of power.

A corollary is that strategic leadership will be more female. Two things are happening: First, women are out-graduating and outperforming men in nearly every important educational category. By raw mental horsepower, that's a leg up to positions where brainpower matters. Second, the way women are perceived by society is changing, from the movies to elite military schools to the selection of the first American female combatant commander. More women will run the strategic show.

Washington's second coming may sport a full tattoo sleeve. The new Grant may prefer sensible earrings to a battlefield cigar. The next Eisenhower may actually be a "Chan" or a "Chavez." When decision superiority matters most, we have to look past haircuts and outfits.

Because there's a timeless quality to strategic leadership. Two hundred fifty years ago, the American idea was in its infancy when a hard British hand grasped its throat. In the same moment, on November 16, 1776, an American ship (the *Andrew Doria*) flying the red-and-white-striped flag of the Continental Congress approached a tiny Dutch island in the West Indes (St. Eustatius). The island's governor, Johannes de Graaff, chose to fire the cannons of Fort Orange in the traditional salute to a foreign vessel entering port. It was the first time, following the Declaration of Independence, that a foreign state recognized an American flag, an American state, and American sovereignty.[8] This was America's first salute.

Without Washington's superior strategic leadership, it might've been America's last (and only) salute. Ever since, every day, Americans and others have needed strategic leadership just as much in so many other walks of life.

And every century or so, it seems we need it again and again to sustain our lives and freedoms. For that reason alone, there are no pursuits more profound than who wins wars and how we change the game.

Now go change yours.

Acknowledgments

I t starts with you. Yes, you. The one reading this now—like, reading these very words. There's nothing easier to do in this world than to put the book down and pick the black brick up. So thank you for coming aboard for this ride, and if you can, please let someone—maybe even me—know what you thought of it all.

For any book to be born, someone must conceive of the idea, but then a lot of others—a whole lot—help bring it into the world. Joe Perry, my agent, believed in it enough to pitch it to the amazing team at Matt Holt Books and BenBella Books, where Katie Dickman and James Fraleigh chainsawed out my worst ideas! This book is better for all of them.

Who Wins Wars began as a doctoral dissertation that would never have been finished without the support of a great host of institutions and individuals. Each deserves high praise, certainly higher than these few words could ever express in such a short space. What follows is merely the down payment on a lifetime of gratitude.

The Modern War Institute at West Point, the Department of Defense & Strategic Studies and Office of the Dean there, and even the Military and Strategic Studies Department at the US Air Force Academy all pitched in with support when I needed it along the way. And the archives and libraries! West Point's Jefferson Library must be considered one of the finest in the world on war, and over the course of 34 months while

"

teaching there, I checked out so many books I lost count (the library, of course, ran the numbers for me: 234). I was also fortunate to visit the Dwight D. Eisenhower Presidential Library in Kansas, the George Washington Presidential Library in Virginia, the University of Utah Library, and the Liddell Hart Centre for Military Archives in London. I also benefited from a US Army War College military staff ride covering the Overland Campaign through Virginia. Additionally, simply living at West Point for nearly three years, amid the ghosts of graduates' past and the cadets of conflict's future, was personally motivating.

I must thank, profusely, Professor Colin Gray for taking me on as a student. I knew him well late in life, from 2013 until his passing in 2020. As an active-duty US Army officer, I was destined to be a distant pupil, but I benefited greatly from his ideas and wisdom. We did not know it at the time, but I was destined to be his final PhD student before illness forced him to let Professor Beatrice Heuser help me cross the finish line. She pushed the pistol away every time I aimed at my foot—I am as deeply indebted to her as Colin.

Due to my military service, aside from many visits to the University of Reading, the bulk of the work was performed while stationed at West Point, in South Korea, and at the US Air Force Academy. As such, I owe thanks to Lieutenant Colonel (ret.) Brian DeToy, PhD, who enthusiastically supported my work through the time he provided me while I taught in his department. In the same category, though not as warmly, it was also helpful that a certain North Korean dictator did not start a war while I served on the Peninsula (which might have seriously hindered the writing process).

While my parents, Barbara and Peter Cavanaugh, gathered the kindling, my daughters Grace and Georgina (*Moibe! Moibesans!*) fueled the fire to finish this dissertation and book every day. Simply put, they make me want to know more and more, and even more, if for no other reason than to be a better father.

Notes

PREFACE

1 Colin S. Gray, *The Strategy Bridge: Theory for Practice* (Oxford University Press, 2010), 205–8.

2 He would later rise to the rank of lieutenant general and serve as the US national security advisor.

3 George Packer, "The Lesson of Tal Afar," *The New Yorker* (April 3, 2006).

4 Paul Yingling, "A Failure in Generalship," *Armed Forces Journal* (May 2007). Reader's Note: This citation was originally accessed online and may no longer be available in that form.

5 Steven Metz, "Strategic Horizons: For U.S. Military, 'Strategic Leadership' Easier Said Than Done," *World Politics Review* (October 24, 2012). Reader's Note: This citation was originally accessed online and may no longer be available in that form.

6 Sarah Sewall, "Soldiers and Citizens: The Military, Politics, and Society in 21st Century America," November 7, 2009, in *Massachusetts Foundation for the Humanities at Boston College*, video, at 14 minutes. Reader's Note: This citation was originally accessed online and may no longer be available in that form.

7 See *Strategy Strikes Back: How* Star Wars *Explains Modern Military Conflict* (University of Nebraska Press, 2020) and *Winning Westeros: How* Game of Thrones *Explains Modern Military Conflict* (University of Nebraska Press, 2019).

8 Much of the following section is based in part on a talk delivered at the US Army War College Annual Strategy Conference (April 24, 2018), "What Will the Generals of 2030 Look Like?"

9 Robert Bracknell, "Book Review," *Joint Forces Quarterly*, Issue 69 (2nd Quarter 2013), 99–100.

10 Jeremy Black, "How Washington Won" (October 3, 2015). *The New York Historical Society*. Audio, at 53 minutes. Reader's Note: This citation was originally accessed online and may no longer be available in that form.

11 Jim Collins and Jerry I. Porras, *Built to Last: Successful Habits of Visionary Companies* (Harper Business, 2004), x. Collins and Porras pioneered the idea of studying two entities, "born in the same era," each with "the same shot in life," looking at them "in comparison" to understand why both "didn't attain the same stature" in the longer run.

12   Sun Tzu, "Weak Points and Strong," *The Art of War*, illustrated and presented by Jessica
     Hagy, *Forbes* (October 17, 2013), https://www.forbes.com/sites/jessicahagy/2013/10/17/
     sun-tzus-the-art-of-war-illustrated-chapter-6/#4d63af1fd12f.

INTRODUCTION

1   David McCullough, *1776* (Simon & Schuster Paperbacks, 2005), 251.
2   David Hackett Fischer, *Washington's Crossing* (Oxford University Press, 2004), 129.
3   Fischer, *Washington's Crossing*, 132.
4   George Washington held the rank of general and commander-in-chief of the Continental
     Army throughout the war (though was sometimes referred to as "Major General") and at
     the end of his life was understood to have held the rank of lieutenant general. As such we
     will use that title in this book. During the war, William Howe held the rank of lieutenant
     general and commander-in-chief of the British Army in North America.
5   Edmund S. Morgan, *The Genius of George Washington* (W. W. Norton, 1980), 3.
6   "General Orders, 2 July 1776," *Washington Papers* vol. 5, 179–82.
7   Alexander George, "Case Studies and Theory Development: The Method of Structured,
     Focused Comparison," in *Diplomacy: New Approaches in History, Theory, and Policy*, ed.
     Paul Gordon Lauren (Free Press, 1979), 40.
8   J. F. C. Fuller, *Generalship: Its Diseases and Their Cure* (Military Service Publishing
     Company, 1936), 78.
9   Lloyd J. Matthews, "The Uniformed Intellectual and His Place in American Arms; Part I:
     Anti-Intellectualism in the Army Yesterday and Today," *Army Magazine* (July 2002), 20.
10   In doing so, this book takes no strong position on the distinction between "decisive"
     and "terminal." In this case, what matters most is that the campaign was the most
     consequential. See Roger J. Spiller, "Six Propositions," in *Between War and Peace: How
     America Ends Its Wars*, ed. Matthew Moten (Free Press, 2011), 18.
11   Colin S. Gray, *The Strategy Bridge: Theory for Practice* (Oxford University Press, 2010), 251.
12   Using Sherman Kent's probability scale devised for the early Central Intelligence
     Agency, "plausible" in this case is defined as odds greater than "almost certainly not,"
     mathematically starting at a range of 7%–12%, and likely higher. See Philip E. Tetlock
     and Dan Gardner, *Superforecasting: The Art and Science of Prediction* (Crown, 2015), 56.
13   See *What If? The World's Foremost Military Historians Imagine What Might Have Been*, ed.
     Robert Cowley (Berkley Books, 2000). See also *What Ifs? of American History: Eminent
     Historians Imagine What Might Have Been*, ed. Robert Cowley (G. P. Putnam's Sons, 2003).
14   Martin van Creveld, *Fighting Power: German and U.S. Army Performance, 1939–1945*
     (Greenwood Press, 1982), 3.

CHAPTER 1

1   Robert Bateman, "There Are Three (and Only Three) Types of Military Strategy," *Esquire*,
     November 30, 2015. Reader's Note: This citation was originally accessed online and may
     no longer be available in that form.
2   See Robert Greene, *The 33 Strategies of War* (Penguin Books, 2007).
3   See ML Cavanaugh, "What Is Strategy?" *Modern War Institute* (November 10, 2016).

4   From *Game of Thrones*, season 2, episode 7 ("A Man Without Honor").

5   Grant, quoted in John Russell Young, *Around the World with General Grant, Vol. 2* (American News Company, 1879), 615.

CHAPTER 2

1   Colin S. Gray, "The Strategist as Hero," *Joint Forces Quarterly* (Issue 62, 3rd Quarter 2011), 37–45.

2   Steven Jermy, "Strategy for Action: Using Force Wisely in the 21st Century," October 26, 2011, in *Ethics, Law and Armed Conflict Programme, Oxford University*, audio, http://podcasts.ox.ac.uk/strategy-action-using-force-wisely-21st-century.

3   Colin S. Gray, *The Strategy Bridge: Theory for Practice* (Oxford University Press, 2010), 197.

4   David Hackett Fischer, *Washington's Crossing* (Oxford University Press, 2004), 132.

5   Fischer, *Washington's Crossing*, 381.

6   Lee to Davis, February 3, 1864, *The Wartime Papers of R.E. Lee*, ed. Clifford Dowdey (Little, Brown, 1961), 666–67.

7   Dwight D. Eisenhower, *Crusade in Europe* (Doubleday, 1948), 246.

8   Paul Kennedy, *Engineers of Victory: The Problem Solvers Who Turned the Tide in the Second World War* (Random House, 2013), 262–63.

9   Adrian Goldsworthy, "Caesar: Diplomacy and Power," *Los Angeles Times* (December 29, 2006).

10   Jack Weatherford, "Genghis Khan: Law and Order," *Los Angeles Times* (December 29, 2006).

11   Joseph J. Ellis, "Washington: The Crying Game," *Los Angeles Times* (December 29, 2006).

12   Harold Holzer, "Lincoln: Focus on the Real Foe," *Los Angeles Times* (December 29, 2006).

13   As it happens, of course, as all were career military, none of these five actually had any facial hair. In this case, shaving habits did not appear to impact their wisdom in any way.

14   J. C. Wylie, *Military Strategy: A General Theory of Power Control* (Naval Institute Press, 1989, originally published 1967), 8–9.

CHAPTER 3

1   Joseph J. Ellis, *Revolutionary Summer: The Birth of American Independence* (Alfred A. Knopf, 2013), 70.

2   Andrew Jackson O'Shaughnessy, *The Men Who Lost America: British Leadership, the American Revolution, and the Fate of the Empire* (Yale University Press, 2013), 92.

3   David Hackett Fischer, *Washington's Crossing* (Oxford University Press, 2004), 381.

4   O'Shaughnessy, *The Men Who Lost America*, 83, 86, 89.

5   O'Shaughnessy, *The Men Who Lost America*, 88.

6   Washington, quoted in O'Shaughnessy, *The Men Who Lost America*, 89.

7   Ken Burns, *The Joe Rogan Experience*, episode #2336 (June 11, 2025).

8   Robert K. Faulkner, "The First American: Book Review of *Washington's Revolution: The Making of America's First Leader* by Robert Middlekauff," *Claremont Review of Books* (Fall 2015), 57; Ron Chernow, *Washington: A Life* (Penguin Press, 2010), 49.

9   Chernow, *Washington: A Life*, 38.

10 George Washington, *The Journal of Major George Washington* (1754). Text, accessed November 17, 2017, available from *Electronic Texts in American Studies*, http://digitalcommons.unl.edu/etas/33.

11 Morgan, *The Genius of George Washington*, 28. See also Chernow, *Washington: A Life*, 289.

12 Eugene E. Prussing, *The Estate of George Washington, Deceased* (Little, Brown, 1927), 418–33.

13 Prussing, *The Estate of George Washington, Deceased.*

14 Prussing, *The Estate of George Washington, Deceased.*

15 Prussing, *The Estate of George Washington, Deceased.*

16 Chernow, *Washington: A Life*, 812.

17 Washington, quoted in Chernow, *Washington: A Life*, 805.

18 Dave R. Palmer, "General George Washington: Grand Strategist or Mere Fabian?," *Parameters* (No. 1, 1974), 2.

19 Palmer, "General George Washington: Grand Strategist or Mere Fabian?," 2.

20 King George III, quoted in David McCullough, *1776* (Simon & Schuster Paperbacks, 2005), 11.

21 King George III, quoted in McCullough, *1776*, 11–12.

22 Lord George Germain, quoted in Piers Mackesy, *The War for America: 1775–1783* (Longmans, Green, 1964), 46.

23 Palmer, "General George Washington: Grand Strategist or Mere Fabian?," 3.

24 Palmer, "General George Washington: Grand Strategist or Mere Fabian?," 3; Fischer, *Washington's Crossing*, 75–77.

25 Fischer, *Washington's Crossing*, 77.

26 Howe, quoted in Fischer, *Washington's Crossing*, 77.

27 Howe, quoted in Fischer, *Washington's Crossing*, 77–78.

28 Troyer Steele Anderson, *The Command of the Howe Brothers During the American Revolution* (Farrar, Straus & Giroux, 1972; reprint of 1936 edition), 121.

29 Germain, quoted in Ellis, *Revolutionary Summer*, 35. Also quoted in Mackesy, *The War for America*, 55.

30 Howe, quoted in Anderson, *The Command of the Howe Brothers During the American Revolution*, 121.

31 Anderson, *The Command of the Howe Brothers During the American Revolution*, 116.

32 O'Shaughnessy, *The Men Who Lost America*, 92.

33 Howe, quoted in Anderson, *The Command of the Howe Brothers During the American Revolution*, 123.

34 Fischer, *Washington's Crossing*, 78–79.

35 Fischer, *Washington's Crossing*, 78–80; Palmer, "General George Washington: Grand Strategist or Mere Fabian?," 4.

36 James D. Scudieri, "Review: *The Men Who Lost America: British Leadership, the American Revolution, and the Fate of the Empire* by Andrew Jackson O'Shaughnessy," *Parameters* 43, no. 4 (Winter 2013–2014), 156.

37 Ellis, *Revolutionary Summer*, xi.

38 Dave R. Palmer, *George Washington's Military Genius* (Regnery History, 2012; originally published as *The Way of the Fox*, Greenwood Press, 1975), 227.

39 O'Shaughnessy, *The Men Who Lost America*, 4. "Had Washington lost this battle in December 1776, the defeat almost certainly would have spelled the end of the revolutionary army and therefore the revolution itself, leaving Britain in control of the North American colonies for an indeterminate period in the future, perhaps as a dependent dominion like Canada." In Paul K. Davis, *100 Decisive Battles: From Ancient Times to the Present* (Oxford University Press, 1999), xi.

40 O'Shaughnessy, *The Men Who Lost America*, 5.

41 "To John Adams from Nathanael Greene, 2 June 1776," Founders Online, National Archives (http://founders.archives.gov/documents/Adams/06-04-02-0100, last update June 29, 2015); *The Adams Papers*, Papers of John Adams, vol. 4, February–August 1776, ed. Robert J. Taylor (Harvard University Press, 1979), 227–31.

42 "From George Washington to Lieutenant Colonel Joseph Reed, 14 January 1776," *Washington Papers* vol. 3, 87–92.

43 "From George Washington to Lund Washington, 30 September 1776," *Washington Papers* vol. 6, 440–443.

44 "From George Washington to Lund Washington, 10–17 December 1776," *Washington Papers* vol. 7, 289–292.

CHAPTER 4

1 Joseph J. Ellis, *Revolutionary Summer: The Birth of American Independence* (Alfred A. Knopf, 2013), x.

2 "John Adams to George Washington, January 1776," quoted in David Hackett Fischer, *Washington's Crossing* (Oxford University Press, 2004), 80.

3 "To George Washington from Major General Charles Lee, 19 February 1776," *Washington Papers* vol. 3, 339–41.

4 "To George Washington from Major General Charles Lee, 29 February 1776," *Washington Papers* vol. 3, 389–93.

5 Ellis, *Revolutionary Summer*, 44, 46.

6 Andrew Jackson O'Shaughnessy, *The Men Who Lost America: British Leadership, the American Revolution, and the Fate of the Empire* (Yale University Press, 2013), 92.

7 Fischer, *Washington's Crossing*, 381.

8 Donald Stoker and Michael W. Jones, "Colonial Military Strategy," in *Strategy in the American War of Independence: A Global Approach*, ed. Donald Stoker, Kenneth J. Hagan, and Michael T. McMaster (Routledge, 2010), 9–10.

9 "General Orders, 2 July 1776," *Washington Papers* vol. 5, 179–82.

10 "From George Washington to Major General Artemas Ward, 9 July 1776," *Washington Papers* vol. 5, 254–56.

11 "From George Washington to John Hancock, 10 July 1776," *Washington Papers* vol. 5, 258–61.

12 "Council of War, 12 July 1776," *Washington Papers*, vol. 5, 280.

13 "From George Washington to John Hancock, 12 August 1776," *Washington Papers* vol. 5, 677–80.

14 David McCullough, *1776* (Simon & Schuster Paperbacks, 2005), 178, 179–80.

15　Jeremy Black, "British Military Strategy," in *Strategy in the American War of Independence: A Global Approach*, ed. Donald Stoker, Kenneth J. Hagan, and Michael T. McMaster (Routledge, 2010), 60.

16　Williamson Murray, "The American Revolution: Hybrid War in America's Past." In *Hybrid Warfare: Fighting Complex Opponents from the Ancient World to the Present*, ed. Williamson Murray and Peter R. Mansoor (Cambridge University Press, 2012), 87; Black, "British Military Strategy," 61, 62.

17　Ellis, *Revolutionary Summer*, 110–11.

18　Collier, quoted in Ellis, *Revolutionary Summer*, 125–26.

19　Charles Stedman, *The History of the Origin, Progress, and Termination of the American War, Volume 1* (P. Wogan, P. Byrne, J. Moore, and W. Jones, 1794), 220.

20　Putnam, quoted in Ellis, *Revolutionary Summer*, 119.

21　Ellis, *Revolutionary Summer*, 173, 183.

22　Henry Clinton, *The American Rebellion: Sir Henry Clinton's Narrative of His Campaigns, 1775–1782, with An Appendix of Original Documents*, ed. William B. Willcox (Yale University Press, 1954), ix.

23　Clinton, *The American Rebellion*, 54.

24　Fischer, *Washington's Crossing*, 381.

25　Clinton, *The American Rebellion*, 55, 56–57.

26　William Howe, *The Narrative of Lieut. Gen. Sir William Howe, in a Committee of the House of Commons, on the 29th of April, 1779, Relative to His Conduct, During His Late Command of the King's Troops in North America, Third Edition* (H. Baldwin, 1779), 5. Text, https://archive.org/details/cihm_20614.

27　Howe, quoted in Fischer, *Washington's Crossing*, 76–77.

28　"Council of War, 29 August 1776," *Washington Papers* vol. 6, 153–55.

29　"From George Washington to John Hancock, 2 September 1776," *Washington Papers* vol. 6, 199–201.

30　"To George Washington from John Hancock, 3 September 1776," *Washington Papers* vol. 6, 207.

31　Ellis, *Revolutionary Summer*, 137.

32　"To George Washington from Nathanael Greene, 5 September 1776," *Washington Papers* vol. 6, 222–24.

33　"From George Washington to John Hancock, 8 September 1776," *Washington Papers* vol. 6, 248–54.

34　"From George Washington to John Hancock, 8 September 1776," *Washington Papers* vol. 6, 248–54.

35　"From George Washington to John Hancock, 8 September 1776," *Washington Papers* vol. 6, 248–54.

36　"From George Washington to John Hancock, 8 September 1776," *Washington Papers* vol. 6, 248–54.

37　"From George Washington to John Hancock, 8 September 1776," *Washington Papers* vol. 6, 248–54.

38   "From George Washington to John Hancock, 14 September 1776," *Washington Papers* vol. 6, 308–9.

39   Fischer, *Washington's Crossing*, 108.

40   Fischer, *Washington's Crossing*, 108.

41   Black, "British Military Strategy," 60.

42   Robertson, quoted in Anderson, *The Command of the Howe Brothers During the American Revolution*, 145.

43   Howe, quoted in Fischer, *Washington's Crossing*, 77.

44   "Henry Strachey Papers: The James S. Copley Library," *Sotheby's* (October 15, 2010). Reader's Note: This citation was originally accessed online and may no longer be available in that form.

45   O'Shaughnessy, *The Men Who Lost America*, 91.

46   Edward G. Lengel, *This Glorious Struggle: George Washington's Revolutionary War Letters*, ed. Edward G. Lengel (HarperCollins, 2007), 53.

47   George Washington, quoted in Lengel, *This Glorious Struggle*, 53–54.

48   Ellis, *Revolutionary Summer*, 78.

49   Henry Strachey, "The Henry Strachey Papers."

50   Black, "British Military Strategy," 62.

51   O'Shaughnessy, *The Men Who Lost America*, 99.

52   Henry Strachey, "The Henry Strachey Papers."

53   Ellis, *Revolutionary Summer*, 134.

54   Henry Strachey, "The Henry Strachey Papers."

55   Howe, *The Narrative of Lieut. Gen. Sir William Howe*, 6.

56   Robert A. Doughty and Ira D. Gruber, eds. *Warfare in the Western World, Volume II: Military Operations Since 1871* (D.C. Heath and Company, 1996), 144.

57   Henry Strachey, "The Henry Strachey Papers."

58   Henry Strachey, "The Henry Strachey Papers."

59   Howe, *The Narrative of Lieut. Gen. Sir William Howe*, 6–7.

60   Fischer, *Washington's Crossing*, 113.

61   Chernow, *Washington: A Life*, 262.

62   Fischer, *Washington's Crossing*, 113–14. See Chernow, *Washington: A Life*, 262, and Washington Irving, *The Life of George Washington* (William L. Allison Co., 1859), 274. Irving claimed he heard the story from an eyewitness; the loss "was said so completely to have overcome him that he wept with the tenderness of a child."

63   Doughty and Gruber, *Warfare in the Western World Vol. 1*, 144.

64   Clinton, *The American Rebellion*, 56.

65   Howe, *The Narrative of Lieut. Gen. Sir William Howe*, 8–9.

66   Fischer, *Washington's Crossing*, 129.

67   Fischer, *Washington's Crossing*, 132.

68   Fischer, *Washington's Crossing*, 135, 184, 185.

69   Stedman, *The History of the Origin, Progress, and Termination of the American War, Volume 1*, 251–52.

70   Robertson, quoted in Fischer, *Washington's Crossing*, 174, 179.

71   Stedman, *The History of the Origin, Progress, and Termination of the American War, Volume 1*, 268.

72   Fischer, *Washington's Crossing*, 381–82.

73   Fischer, *Washington's Crossing*, 383.

74   Fischer, *Washington's Crossing*, 382.

75   "From George Washington to Lund Washington, 30 September 1776," *Washington Papers* vol. 6, 440–43.

76   "Council of War, 6 November 1776," *Washington Papers* vol. 7, 92–93.

77   "From George Washington to John Augustine Washington, 6–19 November 1776," *Washington Papers* vol. 7, 102–6.

78   "From George Washington to Lund Washington, 10–17 December 1776," *Washington Papers* vol. 7, 289–92.

79   "To George Washington from Major General John Sullivan, 13 December 1776," *Washington Papers* vol. 7, 328.

80   "From George Washington to Jonathan Trumbull, Sr., 14 December 1776," *Washington Papers* vol. 7, 340–41.

81   "From George Washington to Lund Washington, 10–17 December 1776," *Washington Papers* vol. 7, 289–92.

82   "From George Washington to John Hancock, 20 December 1776," *Washington Papers* vol. 7, 381–89.

83   "To George Washington from Colonel Joseph Reed, 22 December 1776," *Washington Papers* vol. 7, 414–17.

84   "From George Washington to Colonel Joseph Reed, 23 December 1776," *Washington Papers* vol. 7, 423–24.

85   "From George Washington to the Commanders of the Connecticut and Massachusetts Militias Marching to Peekskill, 24 December 1776," *Washington Papers* vol. 7, 426.

86   "From George Washington to John Hancock, 24 December 1776," *Washington Papers* vol. 7, 429–32.

87   "From George Washington to the Chiefs of the Passamaquoddy Indians, 24 December 1776," *Washington Papers* vol. 7, 433–34.

88   "General Orders, 25 December 1776," *Washington Papers* vol. 7, 434–38.

89   Dave R. Palmer, "General George Washington: Grand Strategist or Mere Fabian?," *Parameters* (No. 1, 1974), 9; Doughty and Gruber, *Warfare in the Western World Vol. 1*, 145; O'Shaughnessy, *The Men Who Lost America*, 102.

CHAPTER 5

1   Ira D. Gruber, *The Howe Brothers and the American Revolution* (Atheneum, 1972), 154.

2   Ron Chernow, *Washington: A Life* (Penguin Press, 2010), 282.

3   Nicholas Cresswell, quoted in Chernow, *Washington: A Life*, 283.

4   From George Washington to Nicholas Cooke, 20 January 1777," Founders Online, National Archives (http://founders.archives.gov/documents/Washington/03-08-02-0121, last update June 29, 2015); *The Papers of George Washington*, Revolutionary War Series, vol.

8, *6 January 1777–27 March 1777*, ed. Frank E. Grizzard Jr. (University Press of Virginia, 1998) [hereafter *Washington Papers*], 113–14.

5   Donald Stoker and Michael W. Jones, "Colonial Military Strategy," in *Strategy in the American War of Independence: A Global Approach*, ed. Donald Stoker, Kenneth J. Hagan, and Michael T. McMaster (Routledge, 2010), 15.

6   "Council of War, 12 July 1776," *Washington Papers* vol. 5, 280.

7   Stoker and Jones, "Colonial Military Strategy," 14–15.

8   "From George Washington to Major General Philip Schuyler, 23 February 1777," *Washington Papers* vol. 8, 433–34.

9   Andrew Jackson O'Shaughnessy, *The Men Who Lost America: British Leadership, the American Revolution, and the Fate of the Empire* (Yale University Press, 2013), 103.

10   Williamson Murray, "The American Revolution: Hybrid War in America's Past." in *Hybrid Warfare: Fighting Complex Opponents from the Ancient World to the Present*, ed. Williamson Murray and Peter R. Mansoor (Cambridge University Press, 2012), 87; Black, "British Military Strategy," 91.

11   Charles Stedman, *The History of the Origin, Progress, and Termination of the American War, Volume 1* (P. Wogan, P. Byrne, J. Moore, and W. Jones, 1794), 270. Text, https://archive.org/details/gri_33125010928733. Robert A. Doughty and Ira D. Gruber, eds., *Warfare in the Western World, Vol. 1: Military Operations from 1600 to 1871* (D. C. Heath 1996), 148.

12   Gruber, *The Howe Brothers*, 157.

13   Robert A. Doughty and Ira D. Gruber, eds. *Warfare in the Western World, Volume II: Military Operations Since 1871* (D. C. Heath and Company, 1996), 146–47.

14   Jeremy Black, "British Military Strategy," in *Strategy in the American War of Independence: A Global Approach*, ed. Donald Stoker, Kenneth J. Hagan, and Michael T. McMaster (Routledge, 2010), 62–63.

15   O'Shaughnessy, *The Men Who Lost America*, 105.

16   Howe, quoted in Gruber, *The Howe Brothers*, 156–57.

17   Black, "British Military Strategy," 64.

18   Black, "British Military Strategy," 63, 65.

19   Black, "British Military Strategy," 66.

20   William Anthony Hay, "Redcoat Leaders Weren't All Dolts," *The National Interest* (July/August 2013), 88.

21   Dave R. Palmer, "General George Washington: Grand Strategist or Mere Fabian?," *Parameters* (No. 1, 1974), 11.

22   James Pritchard, "French Strategy and the American Revolution: A Reappraisal," in *Strategy in the American War of Independence: A Global Approach*, ed. Donald Stoker, Kenneth J. Hagan, and Michael T. McMaster (Routledge, 2010), 144, 146.

23   O'Shaughnessy, *The Men Who Lost America*, 13.

24   See Dave R. Palmer, *George Washington's Military Genius* (Regnery History, 2012; originally published as *The Way of the Fox*, Greenwood Press, 1975); Edmund S. Morgan, *The Genius of George Washington* (W. W. Norton, 1980); Dudley W. Knox, *The Naval Genius of George Washington* (Houghton Mifflin, 1932).

25   Morgan, *The Genius of George Washington*, 6.

26 Joseph J. Ellis, *His Excellency: George Washington* (Alfred A. Knopf, 2004), 271.

27 Chernow, *Washington: A Life*, 292.

28 Palmer, "General George Washington: Grand Strategist or Mere Fabian?," 9.

29 W. T. Sherman, "The Grand Strategy of the War of the Rebellion," *Century Magazine* (February 1888), 591–92.

30 Dwight D. Eisenhower, *Crusade in Europe* (Garden City Books, 1948), 246–47.

31 Jeremy Black, "How Washington Won" (October 3, 2015). *The New York Historical Society*. Audio, at 1 minute.

32 Edward G. Lengel, *General George Washington: A Military Life* (Random House Publishing Group, 2007), xii.

33 Thomas A. Rider II, "George Washington: America's First Soldier," in *A Companion to George Washington*, ed. Edward G. Lengel (Wiley-Blackwell, 2012), 379.

CHAPTER 6

1 Lincoln, quoted in James McPherson, *Tried by War: Abraham Lincoln as Commander in Chief* (Penguin, 2008), 1–2; Abraham Lincoln, *The Collected Works of Abraham Lincoln*, ed. Roy P. Basler (Rutgers University Press, 1953), 1: 509–10.

2 David Allan Johnson, *Decided on the Battlefield: Grant, Sherman, Lincoln and the Election of 1864* (Prometheus Books, 2012), 261.

3 Lincoln, quoted in Geoffrey Ward, Ric Burns, and Ken Burns, *The Civil War* (Vintage Books, 1990), 174.

4 Ulysses S. Grant, *The Personal Memoirs of Ulysses S. Grant: The Complete Annotated Edition*, ed. John F. Marszalek, with David S. Nolen and Louie P. Gallo (The Belknap Press of Harvard University Press, 2017), 476.

5 Charles A. Dana, *Recollections of the Civil War* (D. Appleton and Co., 1902), 210–11. Text, https://archive.org/details/recollectionsofc00danach.

6 T. Harry Williams, *McClellan, Sherman and Grant* (Ivan R. Dee, 1991, reprint 1962 by Rutgers University Press), 81.

7 See "Vice President Francis Underwood" (played by Kevin Spacey), created by Beau Willimon, "House of Cards," *Netflix* (season 2, episode 5, 2014). Dialogue takes place in the woods near Spotsylvania, Virginia, supposedly at the 150th Anniversary of the Overland Campaign.

8 Mark Grimsley, *And Keep Moving On: The Virginia Campaign, May–June 1864* (University of Nebraska Press, 2002), 236.

9 Louis P. Masur, *The Civil War: A Concise History* (Oxford University Press, 2011), 24–25.

10 Obtained from Susan Lintelman, Manuscripts Curator, United States Military Academy Library Circulation Records, *United States Military Academy Library at West Point*, email exchange (May 13, 2015). Note: This list is not exhaustive, and does not indicate the number of times a particular book was renewed.

11 William C. Davis, *Crucible of Command: Ulysses S. Grant and Robert E. Lee—The War They Fought, The Peace They Forged* (Da Capo Press, 2014), 394.

12 Brian Holden Reid, *Robert E. Lee: Icon for a Nation* (Prometheus Books, 2007), 231.

13   Al Kaltman, *The Genius of Robert E. Lee: Leadership Lessons for the Outgunned, Outnumbered and Underfinanced* (Prentice Hall, 2000).

14   Gary W. Gallagher, "'A Great General Is So Rare': Robert E. Lee and the Confederacy," in *Leaders of the Lost Cause: New Perspectives on the Confederate High Command*, ed. Gary W. Gallagher and Joseph T. Glatthaar (Stackpole Books, 2004), 34.

15   John H. Claiborne, quoted in Gallagher, "'A Great General Is So Rare'," 35. See John H. Claiborne, "To My Dear Wife," July 30, 1864, "Letters of John Herbert Claiborne."

16   Thomas Connolly, quoted in Gallagher, "'A Great General Is So Rare'," 35. See Thomas Conolly, *An Irishman in Dixie: Thomas Conolly's Diary of the Fall of the Confederacy*, ed. Nelson D. Lankford (University of South Carolina Press, 1988), 52.

17   Davis, *Crucible of Command*, 394.

18   He graduated twenty-first of thirty-nine, a misleading figure when one considers the class started with eighty-two cadets, half of whom never made it to graduation, which would actually put him closer to the top 25% of his class. Ron Chernow, *Grant* (Penguin, 2017), 23, 27.

19   The issue was that the last person to hold the rank of lieutenant general was George Washington, and a number of politicians were uncomfortable with any other officer holding this title. Brooks Simpson, *Let Us Have Peace: Ulysses S. Grant and the Politics of War and Reconstruction, 1861–1868* (University of North Carolina Press, 1991), 51.

20   See Grimsley, *And Keep Moving On*.

21   Davis, *Crucible of Command*, 393.

22   Masur, *The Civil War*, 25.

23   Reid, *Robert E. Lee*, 198.

24   Ward et al, *The Civil War*, 171–73.

25   Reid, *Robert E. Lee*, 198.

26   Davis, *Crucible of Command*, 393.

27   Interestingly, both passed away at age 63, Lee in 1870 and Grant in 1885.

28   Davis, *Crucible of Command*, 393; Grimsley, *And Keep Moving On*, 145.

29   Donald Stoker, *The Grand Design: Strategy and the U.S. Civil War* (Oxford University Press, 2012), 25.

30   Masur, *The Civil War*, 25.

31   Stoker, *The Grand Design*, 10.

32   Gordon C. Rhea, "'Butcher' Grant and the Overland Campaign." *North & South* Vol. 4, No. 1 (Nov 2000), 44–56; Grimsley, *And Keep Moving On*, 224.

33   Grimsley, *And Keep Moving On*, 236–37.

34   Terry L. Jones, "Could the South Have Won the War?," *New York Times* (March 16, 2015).

35   William W. Freehling, Allen C. Guelzo, Bruce Levine, Richard M. McMurray, James M. McPherson, and Stephen W. Sears, "Could the Confederacy Have Won the Civil War?" *North & South* Vol. 9, No. 2 (May 2006), 13–19.

36   McPherson, "Could the Confederacy Have Won the Civil War?," 17.

37   McMurray, "Could the Confederacy Have Won the Civil War?," 17.

38   James McPherson, "After Words—Embattled Rebel: Jefferson Davis as Commander in

Chief," November 2, 2014, *C-SPAN*, video and audio, at 56 minutes, accessed February 26, 2016, http://www.c-span.org/video/?321903-1/words-james-mcpherson.

39 B. Franklin Cooling, "The Campaign That Could Have Changed the War—and Did: Jubal Early's 1864 Raid on Washington, D.C.," *North & South* Vol. 7, No. 5 (August 2004), 14.

40 Masur, *The Civil War*, 65–66.

41 Lincoln, quoted in Masur, *The Civil War*, 68; Abraham Lincoln, "Memorandum, August 23, 1864," in *The Collected Works of Abraham Lincoln*, 7: 514.

42 Gary W. Gallagher, "Our Hearts Are Full of Hope: The Army of Northern Virginia in the Spring of 1864," in *The Wilderness Campaign*, ed. Gary W. Gallagher (University of North Carolina Press, 1997), 36.

43 Gallagher, "Our Hearts Are Full of Hope," 36, 42.

44 Reid, *Robert E. Lee*, 199.

45 Richard E. Beringer, William N. Still. Jr., Archer Jones, and Herman Hattaway, *Why the South Lost the Civil War* (Georgia University Press, 1986), 424.

46 Longstreet, quoted in McPherson, *Tried By War*, 233. Cites "Entry of June 11, 1864," in *A Rebel War Clerk's Diary at the Confederate States Capital*, ed. Henry Swiggett (Old Hickory Bookshop, 1935), 2: 229. Also cites James Longstreet to Alexander R. Lawton, *O.R. Vol. 32* (March 5, 1864), iii: 588.

47 James McPherson, *Battle Cry of Freedom, The Civil War Era* (Oxford University Press, 1988), 855.

CHAPTER 7

1 Ulysses S. Grant, *The Personal Memoirs of Ulysses S. Grant: The Complete Annotated Edition*, ed. John F. Marszalek, with David S. Nolen and Louie P. Gallo (The Belknap Press of Harvard University Press, 2017), 478, 491.

2 Brooks Simpson, *Let Us Have Peace: Ulysses S. Grant and the Politics of War and Reconstruction, 1861–1868* (University of North Carolina Press, 1991), 54.

3 Grant to Halleck, January 19, 1864, *O.R. Vol. 33*, 394.

4 Halleck to Grant, February 17, 1864, *O.R. Vol. 32/2*, 411–14.

5 Robert E. Lee to Mary Lee, May 23, 1864, *The Wartime Papers of R.E. Lee*, ed. Clifford Dowdey (Little, Brown, 1961), 748.

6 Halleck to Grant, February 17, 1864, *O.R. Vol. 32/2*, 411–14.

7 Grant to Sherman, April 4, 1864, *O.R. Vol. 32/3*, 827.

8 Grant to Sherman, April 4, 1864, *O.R. Vol. 32/3*, 827.

9 Grant to Meade, April 9, 1864, in John Y. Simon, et al., eds., *The Papers of Ulysses S. Grant* [hereafter *PUSG*] (Southern Illinois University Press, 1967–2009), 122: 394–95. Note: Some readers will note this plan's similarities to a Jominian approach to warfare. While it is true that Grant studied Jomini under Dennis Hart Mahan (Alfred Thayer Mahan's father) while a cadet at West Point, Grant also strongly cautioned that slavish observance to military rules was the downfall of many general officers. Therefore, it seems unlikely that Jomini influenced Grant's thought process on this campaign. See Ron Chernow, *Grant* (Penguin, 2017), 23; see also Grant, quoted in John Russell

Young, *Around the World with General Grant, Vol. 2* (American News Company, 1879), 351–53.

10 Simpson, *Let Us Have Peace*, 56–57.

11 Robert E. Lee to Jefferson Davis, February 3, 1864, *The Wartime Papers*, 666–67.

12 Lee, quoted in Brian Holden Reid, *Robert E. Lee: Icon for a Nation* (Prometheus Books, 2007), 197.

13 "Casualties" refers to total numbers of killed, wounded, and missing. Grimsley, *And Keep Moving On*, 226; Reid, *Robert E. Lee*, 205.

14 W. T. Sherman, "The Grand Strategy of the War of the Rebellion," *Century Magazine* (February 1888) 591–92.

15 Grant, quoted in Shelby Foote, *The Civil War: A Narrative, Vol. 3, Red River to Appomattox* (Vintage Books, 1986, 1st ed. 1974), 186.

16 Edward H. Bonekemper III, *Grant and Lee: Victorious American and Vanquished Virginian* (Praeger, 2008), 184.

17 Lincoln, quoted in Brooks D. Simpson, "Great Expectations: Ulysses S. Grant, the Northern Press, and the Opening of the Wilderness Campaign," in *The Wilderness Campaign*, ed. Gary W. Gallagher (University of North Carolina Press, 1997), 19.

18 Bonekemper, *Grant and Lee*, 192. Cites Gordon C. Rhea, *Cold Harbor: Grant and Lee, May 26–June 3, 1864* (Louisiana State University Press, 2002), 382, 386.

19 Grant to Halleck, June 5, 1864, *PUSG*, 11: 19.

20 Grant to Jesse R. Grant, September 5, 1864, *PUSG*, 12: 130.

21 Brooks D. Simpson, "Campaign Promise," *The Civil War Monitor* (Winter 2014), 35.

22 Grant to Halleck, June 5, 1864, *PUSG*, 11: 19.

23 Grant to Halleck, June 5, 1864, *PUSG*, 11: 20.

24 Reid, *Robert E. Lee*, 205–6.

25 Grant, *Memoirs*, 495.

26 Lee to Davis, July 5, 1864, *The Wartime Papers*, 814–15.

27 Grant's order to Sheridan conveyed in dispatch to Halleck. Grant to Halleck, August 1, 1864, *PUSG*, 11: 358.

28 James McPherson, *Tried by War: Abraham Lincoln as Commander in Chief* (Penguin, 2008), 229.

29 Lincoln to Grant, August 3, 1864, *PUSG*, 11: 360n.

30 Louis P. Masur, *The Civil War: A Concise History* (Oxford University Press, 2011), 70.

31 Sheridan, quoted in Geoffrey Ward, Ric Burns, and Ken Burns, *The Civil War* (Vintage Books, 1990), 271.

32 Simpson, "Campaign Promise," 39.

33 Grant to Sherman, September 10, 1864, *PUSG*, 12: 144.

34 Grant to Sherman, October 17, 1864, *PUSG*, 12: 318.

35 Grant to Sheridan, October 14, 1864, *PUSG*, 12: 312.

36 Bonekemper, *Grant and Lee*, 196–97. Alfred C. Young, "Numbers and Losses in the Army of Northern Virginia," *North & South* Vol. 3, No. 3 (March 2000), 19–21.

37 Foote, *The Civil War: A Narrative*, 223, 179, 193, 277; Grimsley, *And Keep Moving On*, 71; Reid, *Robert E. Lee*, 211.

38 Foote, *The Civil War: A Narrative*, 223.

39 Donald Stoker, *The Grand Design: Strategy and the U.S. Civil War* (Oxford University Press, 2012), 364–65.

40 Noah Andre Trudeau, "'A Mere Question of Time': Robert E. Lee from the Wilderness to Appomattox Court House," in *Lee: The Soldier*, ed. Gary W. Gallagher (University of Nebraska Press, 1996), 538.

41 Reid, *Robert E. Lee*, 219–20.

42 References to "losses" or "casualties" means the sum total of killed, wounded, and missing (unless otherwise specified). Foote, *The Civil War: A Narrative*, 146.

43 Gordon C. Rhea, "'Butcher' Grant and the Overland Campaign." *North & South* Vol. 4, No. 1 (Nov 2000), 44–56.

44 Bonekemper, *Grant and Lee*, 189.

45 Simpson, "Great Expectations," 4–5.

46 Grant, *Memoirs*, 510.

47 Bonekemper, *Grant and Lee*, 197.

48 Grant, *Memoirs*, 523.

49 Gary W. Gallagher, "Another Look," in *Lee: The Soldier*, ed. Gary W. Gallagher (University of Nebraska Press, 1996), 280.

50 Gallagher, "Another Look," 281. Cites John Sergeant Wise, *The End of an Era* (Thomas Yoseloff, 1965, originally published 1899), 434.

51 Robert E. Lee to Mary Lee, April 19, 1863, *The Wartime Papers*, 437–38.

52 Lee to Davis, February 3, 1864, *The Wartime Papers*, 666–67.

53 Trudeau, "'A Mere Question of Time'," 523. Cites Robert E. Lee, *The Wartime Papers*, 666–67, 700.

54 Lee to Davis, April 5, 1864, in *The Wartime Papers*, 691.

55 Lee, quoted in Bonekemper, *Grant and Lee*, 187. Cites Gordon C. Rhea, "Robert E. Lee, Prescience, and the Overland Campaign," *North & South* Vol. 3, No. 5 (June 2000), 45.

56 Lee, quoted in Trudeau, "'A Mere Question of Time,'" 533.

57 Lee, quoted in Grimsley, *And Keep Moving On*, 138.

58 Grimsley, *And Keep Moving On*, 138.

59 Lee to Richard H. Anderson, June 4, 1864, *The Wartime Papers*, 765.

60 Grimsley, *And Keep Moving On*, 138.

61 Trudeau, "'A Mere Question of Time,'" 524. Cites Lee to Davis, December 7, 1863, *The Wartime Papers*, 642.

62 Lincoln, quoted in Gallagher, "Another Look," 278. Cites Abraham Lincoln, *The Collected Works of Abraham Lincoln*, ed. Roy P. Basler et al. (Rutgers University Press, 1953), 5: 355–56.

63 Lee to Davis, April 15, 1864, *The Wartime Papers*, 699–700.

64 Lee to Davis, May 4, 1864, *The Wartime Papers*, 719.

65 Robert E. Lee to Mary Lee, May 23, 1864, *The Wartime Papers*, 748.

66 Lee to Davis, May 30, 1864, *The Wartime Papers*, 757.

67 Gallagher, "Another Look," 285, 286, 278.

68 Lee to Braxton Bragg, April 16, 1864, *The Wartime Papers*, 701.

69 This was prior to Sheridan's mission to close the Shenandoah.

70 Larry E. Nelson, *Bullets, Ballots, and Rhetoric: Confederate Policy for the United States Presidential Contest of 1864* (University of Alabama Press, 1980), 1.

71 "By Telegraph for the American & Gazette," *North American and United States Gazette*, Philadelphia, Pennsylvania (July 12, 1864).

72 Reid, *Robert E. Lee*, 222.

73 Reid, *Robert E. Lee*, 227.

74 Lee to A. P. Hill, unrecorded date, May 1864, *The Wartime Papers*, 759–60.

75 Bragg, quoted in Stoker, *The Grand Design*, 370.

76 Lee to Davis, June 11, 1864, *The Wartime Papers*, 774–75.

77 Lee to Davis, June 11, 1864, *The Wartime Papers*, 774–75.

78 Lee to Davis, June 15, 1864, *The Wartime Papers*, 782–83.

79 Jubal A. Early, *A Memoir of the Last Year of the War for Independence in the Confederate States of America* (University of South Carolina Press, 2001), 42, 43, 52.

80 Early, *A Memoir of the Last Year of the War*, 59.

81 Doug Coleman, "Early's Raid on Washington: Monocacy, Fort Stevens and Retaliation in Chambersburg," *Alexandria, Virginia Old Town Crier* (July 2014), 9.

82 Cooling, "Washington's Civil War Defenses and the Battle of Fort Stevens," 28.

83 Lee to Early, July 11, 1864, *The Wartime Papers*, 819.

84 McPherson, *Tried By War*, 226–27.

85 McPherson, *Tried By War*, 224–25.

86 McPherson, *Tried By War*, 226.

87 Cooling, "Washington's Civil War Defenses and the Battle of Fort Stevens," 30.

88 Nelson, *Bullets, Ballots, and Rhetoric*, 60.

89 Grant to Halleck, July 5, 1864, *PUSG*, 11: 170.

90 "Sunday Night's Dispatches," *Milwaukee Daily Sentinel*, Milwaukee, Wisconsin (August 1, 1864).

91 McPherson, *Tried By War*, 225.

92 Grant to Lincoln, July 10, 1864, *PUSG*, 11: 203.

93 Reid, *Robert E. Lee*, 222–23.

94 Simpson, "Campaign Promise," 36.

95 Grant to J. Russell Jones, July 5, 1864, *PUSG*, 11: 176.

96 Grant to Stanton, August 15, 1864, *PUSG*, 11: 421–22.

97 Grant to Elihu Washburne, August 16, 1864, *PUSG*, 11: 423.

98 Lee to Grant, October 1, 1864, *PUSG*, 12: 258.

99 Grant to Lee, October 2, 1864, *PUSG*, 12: 258.

100 Lee to Grant, October 3, 1864, *PUSG*, 12: 263.

101 Grant to Lee, October 3, 1864, *PUSG*, 12: 263.

102 Grant to Stanton, September 13, 1864, *PUSG*, 12: 158–59.

103 Simpson, *Let Us Have Peace*, 59.

104 Grant to Butler, August 18, 1864, *PUSG*, 12: 27.

105 Grant to Seward, August 19, 1864, *PUSG*, 12: 38.

106 Grant, quoted in Young, *Around the World with General Grant*, 447, 615–16.

107 Email exchange with Louis P. Gallo, Publications Editor, Ulysses S. Grant Library and Association, Mississippi State University (September 27, 2016). Grant, quoted in Young, *Around the World with General Grant*, 615–16.

108 David Allan Johnson, *Decided on the Battlefield: Grant, Sherman, Lincoln and the Election of 1864* (Prometheus Books, 2012), 18–19.

109 Grant to Washburne, September 21, 1864, *PUSG*, 12: 185.

110 Grant to Stanton, September 27, 1864, *PUSG*, 12: 212–13.

111 Grant to Stanton, September 27, 1864, *PUSG*, 12: 212–13.

112 Grant to Stanton, September 27, 1864, *PUSG*, 12: 212–13.

113 Grant to Halleck, October 1864, *PUSG*, 12: 317.

114 Grant to Meade, November 5, 1864, *PUSG*, 12: 382.

115 Grant to Alfred H. Terry, November 7, 1864, *PUSG*, 12: 394–95.

116 Stanton to Grant, October 27, 1864, *PUSG*, 12: 353.

117 Grant to Stanton, October 27, 1864, *PUSG*, 12: 353.

118 Grant to Stanton, November 1, 1864, *PUSG*, 12: 353.

119 Grant to Stanton, November 9, 1864, *PUSG*, 12: 395.

120 Abraham Lincoln, Fourth Annual Message to Congress (December 6, 1864).

121 Edward H. Bonekemper III, "Appendix III—The Critical Election of 1864: How Close Was It?" in *Ulysses S. Grant: A Victor, Not a Butcher: The Military Genius of the Man Who Won the Civil War* (Washington: Regnery, 2004), Kindle Edition, Locations 5538, 5541.

122 Bonekemper, *Ulysses S. Grant: A Victor, Not a Butcher*, Kindle Location 5614.

123 Adams, quoted in Masur, *The Civil War*, 72. Cites John C. Waugh, *Reelecting Lincoln: The Battle for the 1864 Presidency* (DaCapo Press, 2001), 357.

124 Lee, quoted in Masur, *The Civil War*, 73. Cites Joseph T. Glatthaar, *General Lee's Army: From Victory to Collapse* (Free Press, 2008), 408.

125 Grant to Stanton, November 10, 1864, *PUSG*, 12: 398.

CHAPTER 8

1 Rhea, "'Butcher' Grant and the Overland Campaign." *North & South* Vol. 4, No. 1 (Nov 2000), 44–56.

2 "Robert E. Lee to James Seddon, August 23, 1864," in *The Wartime Papers of R.E. Lee*, ed. Clifford Dowdey (Little, Brown, 1961), 843–44.

3 "Robert E. Lee to Jefferson Davis, September 2, 1864," *The Wartime Papers*, 847.

4 Sherman and Sheridan's campaigns in 1864 have been called the first instance of modern total war and criticized for being appallingly destructive. While these criticisms may have merit in small, isolated incidents, and Grant's, Sherman's, and Sheridan's rhetoric was indeed rough, the reality is these were largely discriminate campaigns exercised with appropriate discipline. See John B. Walters, *Merchant of Terror: General Sherman and Total War* (Bobbs-Merrill Co., 1973). John F. Marszalek, "Sherman's March and Destructive War," September 18, 2015, at *The New York Historical Society*, audio, at 32 minutes. Reader's Note: This citation was originally accessed online and may no longer be available in that form. See also Jeffry Wert, "'About Played Out': The 1864 Shenandoah Valley Campaign and Its Military and Political Significance," April 8, 2016, at "Atlanta, the

Shenandoah, and the Turn to Total War," conference, video, https://www.c-span.org/video/?407815-3/1864-shenandoah-valley-campaign.

5   Mark Grimsley, *And Keep Moving On: The Virginia Campaign, May–June 1864* (University of Nebraska Press, 2002), 224, 237.

6   Grimsley, *And Keep Moving On*, 225.

7   Wolseley, quoted in W. T. Sherman, "Grant, Thomas, Lee," *The North American Review* Vol. 144, No. 366 (May 1887).

8   Sherman, "Grant, Thomas, Lee," 437, 442, 444.

9   Grant, quoted in John Russell Young, *Around the World with General Grant, Vol. 2* (American News Company, 1879), 351–53.

10   John Rawlins and Charles Francis Adams Jr., quoted in Shelby Foote, *The Civil War: A Narrative, Vol. 3 Red River to Appomattox* (Vintage Books, 1986, 1st ed. 1974), 185–86. Horace Porter, *Campaigning with Grant* (The Century Company, 1897), 71.

11   Frederick D. Grant, "A Boy's Experience at Vicksburg," in A. Noel Blakeman, ed., *Personal Recollections of the War of the Rebellion, Third Series* (G. P. Putnam's Sons, 1907), 96.

12   Grant, quoted in Ron Chernow, *Grant* (Penguin, 2017), 402.

13   David Hackett Fischer, *Washington's Crossing* (Oxford University Press, 2004), 114.

14   Michael Korda, *Ike: An American Hero* (Harper Perennial, 2008), 467. Val Lauder, "Eisenhower's 'Soul-Racking' D-Day decision," *CNN* (June 6, 2014), text, http://edition.cnn.com/2014/06/05/opinion/lauder-eisenhower-d-day-anguish/.

15   Chris Voss, quoted in David Marchese, "This World-Renowned Negotiator Says Trump's Secret Weapon Is Empathy," *New York Times*, https://www.nytimes.com/2025/08/16/magazine/chris-voss-interview.html.

16   Hew Strachan, *The Direction of War: Contemporary Strategy in Historical Perspective* (Cambridge University Press, 2013), 20–21.

17   Nicholas Epley, *Mindwise: Why We Misunderstand What Others Think, Believe, Feel, and Want* (Vintage Books, 2014), 38.

18   Lawrence Freedman, *Strategy: A History* (Oxford University Press, 2013), xii.

19   Amy Chua, *Day of Empire: How Hyperpowers Rise to Global Dominance—and Why They Fall* (Doubleday, 2007), xxi, xxiv.

20   Chua, 330, 336.

21   Gordon Rhea, "Who Were the Top Ten Generals?," *North & South* Vol. 6, No. 4 (May 2003), 16.

22   Geoffrey Ward, Ric Burns, and Ken Burns, *The Civil War* (Vintage Books, 1990), 85, 197, 306.

CHAPTER 9

1   Dwight D. Eisenhower, "[Entry] 1734, June 5, 1944, Note," in *The Papers of Dwight David Eisenhower, The War Years* [Hereafter *"Eisenhower Papers"*]: *III*, ed. Alfred D. Chandler et al. (Johns Hopkins Press, 1970), 1908.

2   Rick Atkinson, "The Road to D-Day: Behind the Battle That Won the War," *Foreign Affairs* Vol. 92, No. 4 (July/August 2013), 75.

3   Douglas Brinkley, "Overlord's Overlord," *New York Times Book Review* of Michael Korda,

Ike: An American Hero (September 30, 2007). Text, http://www.nytimes.com/2007/09/30/books/review/Brinkley-t.html.

4 Jean E. Smith, "Great Generals: General Ulysses S. Grant and the Way We Look at War," December 14, 2013, at *The New York Historical Society*, audio, at 4 minutes. Reader's Note: This citation was originally accessed online and may no longer be available in that form.

5 Andrew Roberts, "Leaders in War: Dwight D. Eisenhower," March 6, 2017, at *The New York Historical Society*, audio, at 20 minutes. Reader's Note: This citation was originally accessed online and may no longer be available in that form.

6 Max Hastings, *Overlord: D-Day and the Battle for Normandy* (Simon & Schuster, 1984), 348.

7 Walter R. Borneman, "The Battle Before the Battles," *Wall Street Journal Book Review* of Jonathan Jordan, *American Warlords: How Roosevelt's High Command Led America to Victory in World War II* (May 23–24, 2015), C9.

8 Roberts, "Leaders in War: Dwight D. Eisenhower," at 37 minutes. Reader's Note: This citation was originally accessed online and may no longer be available in that form.

9 Rick Atkinson, *The Guns at Last Light: The War in Western Europe, 1944–1945, Volume Three of The Liberation Trilogy* (Henry Holt, 2013), 85, 105, 107.

10 Atkinson, *The Guns at Last Light*, 5.

11 Rick Atkinson, "Ten Things Every American Student Should Know About Our Army in World War II," *Foreign Policy Research Institute: Wachman Center for Civic and International Literacy* (August 2012). Text, http://www.fpri.org/article/2012/08/ten-things-every-american-student-should-know-about-our-army-in-world-war-ii/.

12 Heinz Linge, *The Hitler Book*, ed. Henrik Eberle and Matthias Uhl (Bristol Park Books, 2005), 149n.

13 Montgomery and Brooke, quoted in Atkinson, "The Road to D-Day," 64.

14 Stephen A. Hart, "'A Very Lofty Perch': Allied High Command," in *The D-Day Companion: Leading Historians Explore History's Greatest Amphibious Assault*, ed. Jane Penrose (London: Osprey Publishing, 2004), 60.

15 Richard Overy, *Why the Allies Won* (W. W. Norton, 1995), 178–79.

16 Paul Kennedy, *Engineers of Victory: The Problem Solvers Who Turned the Tide in the Second World War* (Random House, 2013), 365, 252.

17 Ian Kershaw, *Fateful Choices: Ten Decisions That Changed the World, 1940–1941* (Penguin Press, 2007), 6.

18 Churchill, quoted in Hastings, *Overlord*, 19.

19 Lieutenant Walter B. Smith, quoted in Samuel Eliot Morison, *Strategy and Compromise: A Reappraisal of the Crucial Decisions Confronting the Allies in the Hazardous Years, 1940–1945* (Little, Brown, 1958), 51–52.

20 Brooke, quoted in Hastings, *Overlord*, 19.

21 "In 1776, a Frederick Eisenhauer [different family name spelling then, which had changed to the modern usage by 1790] . . . was a private in Captain Peter Grubb Jr.'s company of Miles Regiment, which suffered such severe losses in the Battle of Long Island on August 27 that General Washington ordered its reorganization." In Kenneth S. Davis, *Soldier*

of Democracy: A Biography of Dwight Eisenhower (Doubleday, Doran 1945), 12. See also Susan Eisenhower, "How Ike Led," August 20, 2020, *Commonwealth Club of California*, audio, at 23 minutes, https://www.commonwealthclub.org/events/2020-08-19/how-ike-led.

22   Dwight D. Eisenhower, *At Ease: Stories I Tell to Friends* (Eastern National, 2000, reprint 1967), 7. Kenneth S. Davis, *Soldier of Democracy: A Biography of Dwight Eisenhower* (Doubleday, Doran & Company, Inc., 1945), 135.

23   Davis, *Soldier of Democracy*, 146–47.

24   Eisenhower, *At Ease*, 173, 185, 207, 231, 225.

25   Rick Atkinson, "Eisenhower Rising: The Ascent of an Uncommon Man," *Harmon Memorial Lecture, U.S. Air Force Academy* (March 5, 2013), 2.

26   Michael R. Matheny, *Carrying the War to the Enemy: American Operational Art to 1945* (University of Oklahoma Press, 2012), 162.

27   Matheny, *Carrying the War to the Enemy*, 162, 184; Dwight D. Eisenhower, "[Entry] 207, March 25, 1942, *OPD 381* BOLERO, to George Catlett Marshall, *Secret*," *Eisenhower Papers: I*, 205–8.

28   Alan Brooke, "Appointment of Supreme Commanders (Reference C.C.S. (42) 150), Note by the Chief of the Imperial General Staff." See J. Kennedy, 4/6 in Liddell Hart Centre for Military Archives, King's College, London.

29   Matheny, *Carrying the War to the Enemy*, 163, 164.

30   Matheny, *Carrying the War to the Enemy*, 188.

31   Note: "The title COSSAC was used to indicate both the headquarters and its head." Forrest C. Pogue, *United States Army in World War II, The European Theater of Operations: The Supreme Command* (Washington: Chief of Military History, Department of the Army, 1954), 23.

32   Matheny, *Carrying the War to the Enemy*, 189.

33   Hart, "'A Very Lofty Perch': Allied High Command," 51.

34   Walter Bedell Smith, *Eisenhower's Six Great Decisions: Europe 1944–1945* (Longmans, Green, 1956), 12, 15.

35   Stephen R. Taaffe, *Marshall and His Generals: U.S. Army Commanders in World War II* (University Press of Kansas, 2011), 320.

36   Kent Roberts Greenfield, *American Strategy in World War II: A Reconsideration* (Johns Hopkins Press, 1963; reprint Robert E. Krieger Publishing, 1982), 80–83.

37   Overy, *Why The Allies Won*, 274.

38   Williamson Murray, "Who Lost World War II? Was It Hitler? Or the Overrated German General Staff?," *Military History Quarterly* Vol. 26, No. 4 (Summer 2014), 80; Andrew Roberts, *The Storm of War: A New History of the Second World War* (Harper Perennial, 2011), 594, 585.

39   Colin S. Gray, *The Strategy Bridge: Theory for Practice* (Oxford University Press, 2010), 205, 208.

40   Edward Mead Earle, "Hitler: The Nazi Concept of War," in *Makers of Modern Strategy: Military Thought from Machiavelli to Hitler*, ed. Edward Mead Earle (Princeton University Press, 1943), 515.

41   Basil H. Liddell Hart, *The German Generals Talk* (William Morrow), 297–300.

42   Hitler, quoted in Roberts, *The Storm of War*, 578–79.

43   Robert A. Doughty and Ira D. Gruber, eds. *Warfare in the Western World, Volume II: Military Operations Since 1871* (D.C. Heath, 1996), 649.

44   Adolf Hitler, "Führer Directive No. 51" (November 3, 1943). Text, http://ww2db.com/doc.php?q=331.

45   Adolf Hitler, "Evening Situation Report, Probably December 20, 1943," in *Hitler and His Generals: Military Conferences 1942–1945, The First Complete Stenographic Record of the Military Situation Conferences, from Stalingrad to Berlin*, ed. Helmut Heiber and David M. Glantz (Enigma Books, 2003), 314.

46   Hitler, "Evening Situation Report, Probably December 20, 1943," 314, 317.

47   Greenfield, *American Strategy in World War II*, 72, 73, 75.

48   Smith, *Eisenhower's Six Great Decisions*, 15.

49   Atkinson, "The Road to D-Day," 63.

50   Dwight D. Eisenhower, *Crusade in Europe* (Garden City Books, 1948), 228.

51   Eisenhower, *Crusade in Europe*, 217.

52   Bernard L. Montgomery, "First Impressions of Operation OVERLORD," See J. Kennedy, 4/6 in Liddell Hart Centre for Military Archives, King's College, London.

53   Dwight D. Eisenhower, "[Entry] 1497, January 23, 1944, to Combined Chiefs of Staff and British Chiefs of Staff," *Eisenhower Papers: III*, 1673–76.

54   Friedrich Ruge, "The Invasion of Normandy," in *Decisive Battles of World War II: The German View*, ed. H. A. Jacobsen and J. Rohwer, trans. Edward Fitzgerald (G. P. Putnam's Sons, 1965), 317, 319. Note: From November 1943 to August 1944, Ruge served as naval advisor to Field Marshal Rommel.

55   Ruge, "The Invasion of Normandy," 321, 323.

56   Dennis Showalter, "'Throw Them Back,' German Planning and Command," in *The D-Day Companion: Leading Historians Explore History's Greatest Amphibious Assault*, ed. Jane Penrose (Osprey Publishing, 2004), 68–70.

57   Hitler, "Füehrer Directive 51."

58   Showalter, "'Throw Them Back,' German Planning and Command," 70–71.

59   *D-Day 360*, directed by Ian Duncan (U.S. Public Broadcasting Service, 2014), video, at 4, 24, and 25 minutes.

60   See Robert Cowley, *What If? The World's Foremost Military Historians Imagine What Might Have Been* (G. P. Putnam's Sons, 1999); David Fromkin, "Triumph of the Dictators," in Robert Cowley, *What If? The World's Foremost Military Historians Imagine What Might Have Been* (G. P. Putnam's Sons, 1999), 308; John Keegan, "How Hitler Could Have Won The War," in Robert Cowley, *What If? The World's Foremost Military Historians Imagine What Might Have Been* (G. P. Putnam's Sons, 1999), 295.

61   Stephen E. Ambrose, "D-Day Fails: Atomic Alternatives in Europe," in Robert Cowley, *What If? The World's Foremost Military Historians Imagine What Might Have Been* (G. P. Putnam's Sons, 1999), 341, 346, 347.

62   Showalter, "'Throw Them Back,' German Planning and Command," 73.

63   Basil H. Liddell Hart, "What Are Hitler's Generals Thinking?" *The Daily Mail* (July 5, 1943). Liddell Hart Military Archives, in 10/1943/30b.

64   Ken Maurer, "U.S. Naval War College Lecture," December 16, 2013, at The U.S. Naval War College, audio, at 24 minutes. Reader's Note: This citation was originally accessed online and may no longer be available in that form.

65   Morison, *Strategy and Compromise*, 59–60.

66   Brendan Simms, "Comrades in Arms: Book Review of *The Devils' Alliance* by Roger Moorhouse," *Wall Street Journal* (December 1, 2014), A15.

67   Adolf Hitler, "Evening Situation Report, Probably December 20, 1943," 314.

CHAPTER 10

1   Dwight D. Eisenhower, "[Entry] 1601, March 22, 1944, Memorandum, *Secret*," *Eisenhower Papers: III*, 1782–87.

2   Dwight D. Eisenhower, "[Entry] 1474, January 5, 1944, To Carl Spaatz, *Secret*," *Eisenhower Papers: III*, 1654.

3   Michael R. Matheny, *Carrying the War to the Enemy: American Operational Art to 1945* (University of Oklahoma Press, 2012), 193.

4   John E. Fagg, "Plan for OVERLORD" in *The Army Air Forces in World War II, Vol. 3, Europe: Argument to V-E Day, January 1944 to May 1945* (University of Chicago Press, 1951), 72–73.

5   Harry C. Butcher, *My Three Years with Eisenhower: The Personal Diary of Captain Harry C. Butcher, USNR, Naval Aide to General Eisenhower, 1942 to 1945* (Simon & Schuster, 1946), 507.

6   Fagg, "Plan for OVERLORD," 73.

7   Fagg, "Plan for OVERLORD," 73.

8   Fagg, "Plan for OVERLORD," 73–74.

9   Fagg, "Plan for OVERLORD," 75–76.

10   Spaatz plan, quoted in Fagg, "Plan for OVERLORD," 75–76, 78.

11   Fagg, "Plan for OVERLORD," 77.

12   Matheny, *Carrying the War to the Enemy*, 193; Fagg, "Plan for OVERLORD," 78.

13   Dwight D. Eisenhower, "[Entry] 1630, April 5, 1944, to Winston Spencer Churchill, *Top Secret*," *Eisenhower Papers: III*, 1809–10.

14   Walter Bedell Smith, *Eisenhower's Six Great Decisions: Europe 1944–1945* (Longmans, Green and Co., 1956), 38.

15   Dwight D. Eisenhower, "[Entry] 1658, April 29, 1944, to George Catlett Marshall, *Secret*," *Eisenhower Papers: III*, 1838–39.

16   Dwight D. Eisenhower, "[Entry] 1662, May 2, 1944, to Winston Spencer Churchill, *Top Secret*," *Eisenhower Papers: III*, 1842–45.

17   Eisenhower, "[Entry] 1662, May 2, 1944, to Winston Spencer Churchill, *Top Secret*," *Eisenhower Papers: III*, 1842–1845.

18   Paul Kennedy, *Engineers of Victory: The Problem Solvers Who Turned the Tide in the Second World War* (Random House, 2013), 134.

19 See "Note" at Dwight D. Eisenhower, "[Entry] 1630, April 5, 1944, to Winston Spencer Churchill, *Top Secret*," *Eisenhower Papers: III*, 1809–10.

20 Hitler, quoted in Heinz Linge, *The Hitler Book*, ed. Henrik Eberle and Matthias Uhl (Bristol Park Books, 2005), 148–49.

21 Kennedy, *Engineers of Victory*, 258.

22 Friedrich Ruge, "The Invasion of Normandy," in *Decisive Battles of World War II: The German View* ed. H. A. Jacobsen and J. Rohwer, trans. Edward Fitzgerald (G. P. Putnam's Sons, 1965), 317.

23 Dennis Showalter, "'Throw Them Back,' German Planning and Command," in *The D-Day Companion: Leading Historians Explore History's Greatest Amphibious Assault*, ed. Jane Penrose (Osprey Publishing, 2004), 77–78.

24 Showalter, "'Throw Them Back,' German Planning and Command," 66, 68–71.

25 Showalter, "'Throw Them Back,' German Planning and Command," 75.

26 Showalter, "'Throw Them Back,' German Planning and Command," 72–73.

27 Showalter, "'Throw Them Back,' German Planning and Command," 73–74; Kennedy, *Engineers of Victory*, 262.

28 Kennedy, *Engineers of Victory*, 76, 262–63.

29 Andrew Roberts, *The Storm of War: A New History of the Second World War* (Harper Perennial, 2011), 594.

30 Ruge, "The Invasion of Normandy," 323, 472.

31 Gunther Blumentritt, "Report of the Chief of Staff," in *Fighting the Invasion: The German Army at D-Day by Gunther Blumentritt, Wilhelm Keitel, Alfred Jodl, Walter Warlimont, Freiherr von Luttwitz et al.*, ed. David C. Isby (Stackpole Books, 2000), 19.

32 Ruge, "The Invasion of Normandy," 336–37. Blumentritt, "Report of the Chief of Staff," 29.

33 Ruge, "The Invasion of Normandy," 337.

34 Matheny, *Carrying the War to the Enemy*, 190.

35 George C. Marshall, "To Dwight D. Eisenhower, February 10, 1944," in *The Papers of George Catlett Marshall* [hereafter "*Marshall Papers*"], *Volume 4: "Aggressive and Determined Leadership," June 1, 1943–December 31, 1944*, ed. Larry I. Bland and Sharon Ritenour Stevens (Johns Hopkins Press, 1996), 282.

36 Marshall, "To Dwight D. Eisenhower, February 10, 1944," *Marshall Papers, Vol. 4*, 283.

37 Marshall, "To Dwight D. Eisenhower, February 10, 1944," *Marshall Papers, Vol. 4*, 283.

38 Matheny, *Carrying the War to the Enemy*, 190–91.

39 Dwight D. Eisenhower, "[Entry] 1558, February 19, 1944, to George Catlett Marshall, *Secret*," *Eisenhower Papers: III*, 1736–40.

40 Dwight D. Eisenhower, "[Entry] 1558, February 19, 1944, to George Catlett Marshall, *Secret*," *Eisenhower Papers: III*, 1736–40.

41 Butcher, *My Three Years with Eisenhower*, 551.

42 Dwight D. Eisenhower, *The Eisenhower Diaries*, ed. Robert H. Ferrell (W. W. Norton & Company, 1981),117.

43 Allan R. Millett, "Blood Upon the Risers: 'Airborne,'" in *The D-Day Companion: Leading Historians Explore History's Greatest Amphibious Assault*, ed. Jane Penrose (Osprey Publishing,

2004), 126; Trafford Leigh-Mallory, quoted in "Note," Dwight D. Eisenhower, "[Entry] 1720, May 30, 1944, to Trafford Leigh-Mallory, *Top Secret*," *Eisenhower Papers: III*, 1895.

44 Eisenhower, *Crusade in Europe*, 246.

45 Smith, *Eisenhower's Six Great Decisions*, 18, 35.

46 Eisenhower, *Crusade in Europe*, 246.

47 Eisenhower, *Crusade in Europe*, 246.

48 Eisenhower, *Crusade in Europe*, 246.

49 Eisenhower, *Crusade in Europe*, 246–47.

50 Eisenhower, *Crusade in Europe*, 246–47.

51 Eisenhower, *Crusade in Europe*, 246–47.

52 Dwight D. Eisenhower, "[Entry] 1720, May 30, 1944, To Trafford Leigh-Mallory, *Top Secret*," *Eisenhower Papers: III*, 1894–95.

53 Val Lauder, "Eisenhower's 'Soul-Racking' D-Day Decision," CNN (June 6, 2014). Text, http://edition.cnn.com/2014/06/05/opinion/lauder-eisenhower-d-day-anguish/. Note: Eisenhower's granddaughter, Susan Eisenhower, has written that the figures were actually "4 percent overall and about 10 percent on the first day of action." Susan Eisenhower, *How Ike Led: The Principles Behind Eisenhower's Biggest Decisions* (Thomas Dunne Books, 2020), 33.

54 Eisenhower, *Crusade in Europe*, 247.

55 Steven J. Zaloga, *German V-Weapon Sites, 1943–45* (Osprey Publishing, 2007), 18, 9.

56 "V-Weapon," *Vergeltungswaffe* in German, means "reprisal weapon." Hitler, quoted in Roberts, *The Storm of War*, 514–18. See also *Hitler and His Generals*, ed. Heiber and Glantz, 188.

57 Zaloga, *German V-Weapon Sites*, 58–59.

58 Joseph W. Angell, "CROSSBOW," in *The Army Air Forces in World War II, Vol. 3, EUROPE: ARGUMENT TO V-E DAY, JANUARY 1944 TO MAY 1945* (University of Chicago Press, 1951), 84.

59 Butcher, *My Three Years with Eisenhower*, 586.

60 Roberts, *The Storm of War*, 516–17; Angell, "CROSSBOW," 84.

61 Zaloga, *German V-Weapon Sites*, 58.

62 Roberts, *The Storm of War*, 516.

63 Butcher, *My Three Years with Eisenhower*, 587–88.

64 Roberts, *The Storm of War*, 516–17.

65 Zaloga, *German V-Weapon Sites*, 58.

66 Rick Atkinson, *The Guns at Last Light: The War in Western Europe, 1944–1945, Volume Three of The Liberation Trilogy* (Henry Holt and Company, 2013), 196, 199.

67 William B. Breuer, *Operation Dragoon: The Allied Invasion of the South of France* (Presidio Press, 1987), 249.

68 Brooke, quoted in Atkinson, *The Guns at Last Light*, 192.

69 Atkinson, *The Guns at Last Light*, 192; Dwight D. Eisenhower, "[Entry] 1755, June 16, 1944, to Henry Maitland Wilson, *Top Secret*," *Eisenhower Papers: III*, 1930–31.

70 Eisenhower, "[Entry] 1755, June 16, 1944, to Henry Maitland Wilson, *Top Secret*," *Eisenhower Papers: III*, 1931.

71   Eisenhower, "[Entry] 1755, June 16, 1944, to Henry Maitland Wilson, *Top Secret*," *Eisenhower Papers: III*, 1931.

72   Eisenhower, "[Entry] 1755, June 16, 1944, to Henry Maitland Wilson, *Top Secret*," *Eisenhower Papers: III*, 1931.

73   Dwight D. Eisenhower, "[Entry] 1765, June 20, 1944, to George Catlett Marshall, *Top Secret*," *Eisenhower Papers: III*, 1938.

74   Eisenhower, "[Entry] 1765, June 20, 1944, to George Catlett Marshall, *Top Secret*," *Eisenhower Papers: III*, 1938.

75   Dwight D. Eisenhower, "[Entry] 1770, June 23, 1944, to Combined Chiefs of Staff, *Top Secret*," *Eisenhower Papers: III*, 1943–46.

76   Dwight D. Eisenhower, "[Entry] 1770, June 23, 1944, to Combined Chiefs of Staff, *Top secret*," *Eisenhower Papers: III*, 1943–46.

77   Churchill, quoted in note in Dwight D. Eisenhower, "[Entry] 1785, June 29, 1944, to George Catlett Marshall, *Top Secret*," *Eisenhower Papers: III*, 1959–60.

78   Roosevelt, quoted in note in Eisenhower, "[Entry] 1785, June 29, 1944, to George Catlett Marshall, *Top Secret*," *Eisenhower Papers: III*, 1959–60.

79   Roosevelt, quoted in note in Eisenhower, "[Entry] 1785, June 29, 1944, to George Catlett Marshall, *Top Secret*," *Eisenhower Papers: III*, 1959–60. See also Winston S. Churchill, "Appendix D, Book One," *The Second World War, Volume 6: Triumph and Tragedy* (Houghton Mifflin Company), 716–23.

80   Eisenhower, *The Eisenhower Diaries*, 123–25.

81   Atkinson, *The Guns at Last Light*, 194, 216, 213, 192, 219, 175; Weinberg, *A World At Arms*, 761n; Pogue, *United States Army in World War II, The European Theater of Operations: The Supreme Command*, 226; Andrew Roberts, "Leaders in War: Charles de Gaulle," January 19, 2016, at The New York Historical Society, audio. Reader's Note: This citation was originally accessed online and may no longer be available in that form.

82   Kennedy, *Engineers of Victory*, 277.

83   Alan F. Wilt, *The Atlantic Wall, 1941–1944: Hitler's Defenses for D-Day* (Enigma Books, 2004), 137.

84   Rommel's views represented by Atkinson, *The Guns at Last Light*, 105–6.

85   Atkinson, *The Guns at Last Light*, 85.

86   Michael O'Hanlon, "Why China Cannot Conquer Taiwan," *International Security* Vol. 25, No. 2 (Autumn 2000), 54.

87   Atkinson, *The Guns at Last Light*, 106.

88   Kennedy, *Engineers of Victory*, 277.

89   Atkinson, *The Guns at Last Light*, 106.

90   Roberts, *The Storm of War*, 595.

91   Hitler, quoted in Wilt, *The Atlantic Wall*, 138–39.

92   Wilt, *The Atlantic Wall*, 139.

93   *D-Day 360*, at 44 minutes.

94   Wilt, *The Atlantic Wall*, 138–39.

95   Len Fullenkamp, quoted in *D-Day 360*, at 27 minutes.

96 Wilt, *The Atlantic Wall*, 138.

97 Wilt, *The Atlantic Wall*, 137–38. See also Linge, *The Hitler Book*, 161.

98 Roberts, *The Storm of War*, 595.

99 Sungmin Cho, "Anticipating and Preparing for the Potential Assassination of Kim Jong-Un," *International Journal of Korean Studies*, Vol. XIX, No. 1 (Spring/Summer 2015), 179–80; Linge, *The Hitler Book*, 161n.

100 Wilt, *The Atlantic Wall*, 137–38.

101 Wilt, *The Atlantic Wall*, 138.

102 Beyerlein, quoted in Atkinson, *The Guns at Last Light*, 181.

CHAPTER 11

1 Max Hastings, *Overlord: D-Day and the Battle for Normandy* (Simon & Schuster, 1984), 11.

2 Colin S. Gray, *The Strategy Bridge: Theory for Practice* (Oxford University Press, 2010), 251.

3 Rick Atkinson, *The Guns at Last Light: The War in Western Europe, 1944–1945, Volume Three of The Liberation Trilogy* (Henry Holt, 2013), 110, 107.

4 Kenneth S. Davis, *Soldier of Democracy: A Biography of Dwight Eisenhower* (Doubleday, Doran & Company, 1945), 541–42.

5 Douglas Brinkley, "Overlord's Overlord," *New York Times Book Review* of Michael Korda, *Ike: An American Hero* (September 30, 2007). Text, http://www.nytimes.com/2007/09/30/books/review/Brinkley-t.html. Brinkley wrote, "false humility . . . was Eisenhower's greatest stratagem," and Brinkley advised readers to disregard the "cartoonish image of the 'nice guy' general," that "Eisenhower was always ready to cut down anybody who got in his way."

6 Andrew Carroll, "My Fellow Soldiers," August 11, 2017, at the Pritzker Military Museum and Library, audio and text, at 52 minutes, https://www.pritzkermilitary.org/whats_on/pritzker-military-presents/andrew-carroll-my-fellow-soldiers/; Susan Eisenhower, *How Ike Led* (Thomas Dunne Books, 2020), 17.

7 Walter Bedell Smith, *Eisenhower's Six Great Decisions: Europe 1944–1945* (Longmans, Green and Co., 1956) 229.

8 Dwight D. Eisenhower, *At Ease: Stories I Tell to Friends* (Eastern National, 2000, reprint 1967), 298, 300; Rick Atkinson, "Eisenhower Rising: The Ascent of an Uncommon Man," *Harmon Memorial Lecture, U.S. Air Force Academy* (March 5, 2013) 8.

9 Jayson Jenks, "Josh Johnson Has Played for a Record Number of NFL Teams. What Has He Learned About Leadership?" *The Athletic* (August 1, 2025), https://www.nytimes.com/athletic/6527336/2025/08/01/josh-johnson-nfl-leadership/.

10 Eisenhower, *At Ease*, 168, 173.

11 Eisenhower, *At Ease*, 185–86.

12 Eisenhower, *At Ease*, 185–86.

13 Davis, *Soldier of Democracy*, 225–26.

14 Eisenhower, *At Ease*, 225, 227–28.

15 Churchill, quoted in Eisenhower, *At Ease*, 274.

CHAPTER 12

1   Ron Chernow, *Washington: A Life* (Penguin Press, 2010), 29. Ron Chernow, *Grant* (Penguin, 2017), 19, 26, 27. Dwight D. Eisenhower, *At Ease: Stories I Tell to Friends* (Eastern National, 2000, reprint 1967), 7.

2   Stephen E. Ambrose, *The Supreme Commander: The War Years of Dwight D. Eisenhower* (Anchor, 2012), 55, 271. "From George Washington to Lund Washington, 10–17 December 1776," *Washington Papers* vol. 7, 289–92.

3   Rick Atkinson, "Eisenhower Rising: The Ascent of an Uncommon Man," *Harmon Memorial Lecture, U.S. Air Force Academy* (March 5, 2013), 7.

4   J. F. C. Fuller, *Generalship: Its Diseases and Their Cure* (Military Service Publishing Company, 1936), 97–98. Grant, quoted in John Russell Young, *Around the World with General Grant, Vol. 2* (American News Company, 1879), 352–53.

5   Andy Harris, "Young, Brilliant and Underfunded," *New York Times* (October 2, 2014).

6   Chernow, *Washington: A Life*, xix–xx; Chernow, *Grant*, 402. Stephen R. Taaffe, *Marshall and His Generals: U.S. Army Commanders in World War II* (University Press of Kansas, 2011), 55.

7   Edmund S. Morgan, *The Genius of George Washington* (W. W. Norton, 1980), 10, 13. Grant, quoted in Young, *Around the World with General Grant*, 447, 615–16; Kenneth S. Davis, *Soldier of Democracy: A Biography of Dwight Eisenhower* (Doubleday, Doran & Company, Inc., 1945), 191; Stephen E. Ambrose, *Eisenhower: Soldier and President* (Simon & Schuster, 2014, rev. ed.), 208–09.

8   Joseph J. Ellis, *His Excellency: George Washington* (Alfred A. Knopf, 2004), 188.

9   H. W. Brands, *The Man Who Saved the Union: Ulysses Grant in War and Peace* (Doubleday, 2012), 636.

10 Ambrose, *Eisenhower: Soldier and President*, 12.

11 Carl von Clausewitz, *On War*, ed. and trans. Michael Howard and Peter Paret. (Princeton University Press), 1976, 75, 605.

12 Gideon Rose, *How Wars End: Why We Always Fight the Last Battle* (Simon & Schuster, 2010), 3.

13 Barry Strauss, "America 2016: What Does the World Think?" *CNN Global Public Square with Fareed Zakaria*, March 13, 2016, audio, at 27 minutes, https://transcripts.cnn.com/show/fzgps/date/2016-03-13/segment/01.

14 William M. Ferraro, "George Washington's Mind," in *A Companion to George Washington*, ed. Edward G. Lengel (Wiley-Blackwell, 2012), 548.

15 John Marszalek, "Introduction" in Ulysses S. Grant, *The Personal Memoirs of Ulysses S. Grant*, xxv–xxvi.

16 Eugene E. Prussing, *The Estate of George Washington, Deceased* (Little, Brown, 1927), 418–33.

17 Grant, quoted in Young, *Around the World with General Grant*, 450–51.

18 Fuller, *Grant and Lee*, 66–67.

19 Ambrose, *The Supreme Commander*, 55.

20 Ellis, *His Excellency*, 8–10.

21 Chernow, *Grant*, 18, 12, 17.

22 Victor Geortzel et al., *Cradles of Eminence, 2nd Edition: Childhoods of More than 700 Famous Men and Women* (Great Potential Press, 2004, originally published 1962), 64–65.

23 Geortzel et al., *Cradles of Eminence*, vii.

24 Geortzel et al., *Cradles of Eminence*, 282–83.

25 Meg Jay, "The Secrets of Resilience," *Wall Street Journal* (Saturday/Sunday, November 11–12, 2017), C1.

26 Winston Churchill, *The River War: An Historical Account of the Reconquest of the Soudan* (1899), cited by Andrew Roberts, "Winston Churchill: Walking with Destiny," January 16, 2018, at The New York Historical Society, audio, at 19 minutes. Reader's Note: This citation was originally accessed online and may no longer be available in that form.

27 2018 interview with Fox Business, quoted in Sebastian Herrera, "At 81, Larry Ellison Is More Interesting than Ever," *Wall Street Journal*, September 13, 2025.

28 Ulysses S. Grant, *The Personal Memoirs of Ulysses S. Grant: The Complete Annotated Edition*, ed. John F. Marszalek, with David S. Nolen and Louie P. Gallo (The Belknap Press of Harvard University Press, 2017), 175.

29 Herman Kahn and Irwin Mann, "War Gaming," *Rand* (1957), https://www.rand.org/pubs/papers/P1167.html.

30 Eisenhower, *At Ease*, 255.

31 Eisenhower, *At Ease*, 264–65.

32 History, of course, does feature some pretty interesting moments where certain inventions were invented on separate continents at roughly the same time . . . but that's not what we're talking about here.

33 See ML Cavanaugh, "Why America Needs Optimistic Generals," Modern War Institute (September 6, 2018).

34 "From George Washington to Lund Washington, 10–17 December 1776," *Washington Papers* vol. 7, 289–92.

35 Grant to Elihu Washburne, August 16, 1864, *The Papers of Ulysses S. Grant* (Southern Illinois University Press, 1967–2009), 11: 423.

CHAPTER 13

1 Aurelien Breeden, "Napoleon's Hat, Dropped at Waterloo, Is Picked Up at Auction for $400,000," *New York Times* (June 18, 2018).

2 Darrin McMahon, *Divine Fury: A History of Genius* (Basic Books, 2013), 229–30.

3 McMahon, *Divine Fury*, 229–30.

4 McMahon, *Divine Fury*, 229–30.

5 Donald Kagan, *Thucydides: The Reinvention of History* (Penguin Books, 2009), 8.

6 Eliot A. Cohen, *Conquered into Liberty: Two Centuries of Battles Along the Great Warpath That Made the American Way of War* (Free Press, 2011), 222.

7 See Stanley McChrystal, "Public Lecture: My Share of the Task," Pritzker Military Library (Chicago, unpublished, February 25, 2013), video, https://www.youtube.com/watch?v=M7k9hZDCj8I.

8 Barbara W. Tuchman, *The First Salute: A View of the American Revolution* (Knopf, 1988), 5–6.

Index

About the Author

ML (Matt) Cavanaugh, PhD, is a West Point graduate, retired lieutenant colonel and US Army Strategist who earned two Bronze Star Medals and the Combat Action Badge while fighting with the Third Armored Cavalry Regiment.

Matt co-founded the Modern War Institute at West Point, has been the youngest recipient of the Army Strategist Association's professional award—the Order of Saint Gabriel the Archangel—and earned acclaim as the top professor at West Point. He earned a Master of Strategic Studies from Victoria University in Wellington, New Zealand, and a PhD in International Relations from the University of Reading in the United Kingdom.

Selected US Army Athlete of the Year in 2009, Matt holds the record as the fastest American ever to race the 4 Deserts Grand Slam series—twice named by *Time* as one of the world's toughest endurance races, alongside the Tour de France—and he won The Last Desert, the longest ultramarathon across Antarctica, in 2022, a feat accomplished not long after he became a living kidney donor. His book *Best Scar Wins: How You Can Be More Than You Were Before* recounts this experience.

A contributor to *The Los Angeles Times*, his writing has also been featured in *The New York Times*, *Washington Post*, *Wall Street Journal*, *USA Today*, and *The Sydney Morning Herald*, among others. As a sought-after public and motivational speaker based in Colorado, Matt has shared insights with large and small companies, medical and healthcare organizations, sports teams, and students across the country. For more, please visit MLCavanaugh.com or WhoWinsWars.com.